LIVING WORDS IN I CORINTHIANS

Wayne Detzler

 EVANGELICAL PRESS

EVANGELICAL PRESS
16/18 High Street, Welwyn, Hertfordshire,
AL6 9EQ, England.

© Evangelical Press 1983

First published 1983

ISBN 0 85234 177 6

Bible quotations are from the
New International Version

Also available in this series by Wayne Detzler:
LIVING WORDS IN EPHESIANS
LIVING WORDS IN 1 PETER

Cover design by Peter Wagstaff
Typeset in Great Britain by Solo Typesetting, Maidstone
Printed in the USA

To Dr Earle E. Cairns
who first opened to me the treasures of
1 Corinthians

Contents

Preface

Tackling the First Epistle to the Corinthians is like Daniel taking a holiday in the lions' den. No single book in the New Testament is more crowded with predatory problems than this one, and any one of them can attack the Christian community.

It is therefore with no sense of smugness that I present *Living Words in 1 Corinthians*. Despite the dangers of delving into this Pauline letter, its rewards have been great. It is my prayer that the reader will likewise collect the prize for wrestling with the doctrinal lions of 1 Corinthians.

Again my thanks must be expressed to Margaret, my long-suffering spouse, who not only listens to my preaching, but also proof-reads my writing. Mrs Vi Williams takes the very rough draft from me and makes it presentable for publication, and to her also I am deeply indebted.

Most of all I thank you for taking time to read these notes from 1 Corinthians.

Wayne Detzler
Bristol
1983

1.
He is Lord

Almost every language has a word for 'lord'. The Scots speak of the 'laird'. In Germany he is the *Herr*. Meanwhile many Latin languages have variants of *señor*. 'Lord' in any language used to strike terror into peasants' hearts. Now it is just a form, a term of respect, and sometimes even of ridicule.

In 1 Corinthians 1:1-9 the word 'Lord' appears six times. In each case it refers to Jesus Christ. The Greek word behind the English is *kyrios*. We see it in liturgical chants such as *kyrie eleison* ('Lord, have mercy').

Paul introduces this monumental title by a personal reference. In 1 Corinthians 1:2 he speaks of 'our Lord'. The Christian is related by grace through faith to Jesus Christ. This initiates a totally new relationship as Christ becomes our Lord. But there is also an extended relationship, because others own him as Lord. So we are related to one another: he is 'our Lord and theirs' (1 Cor. 1:2).

Jesus Christ is the Great Leveller. Once we submit to his lordship, we are drawn into a relationship with all who submit to him as Lord. Consider the negative and positive implications of this relationship.

Negatively, there can be no narrowness in Christ. I cannot exclude those who are not personally pleasing to me. There is also no bigotry in fellowship under the Lord. When other races or economic classes are represented in my church, I dare not recoil from sitting next to them or speaking to them. Neither is there a sense of superiority in this relationship. A rich Christian is not superior to the poor one, neither is the educated revered above the uneducated.

Another appearance of our word is in verse 3, where we have the full name: 'the Lord Jesus Christ'. Here is relationship within the Godhead. The Lord Jesus Christ is the Son in contradistinction to God the Father. However, this does not only instruct us in trinitarian relationship, it also sets out the credentials of the Lord. He is Lord because he made all things (John 1:3). He is Lord because he upholds all things (Heb. 1:3). He is Lord because of his saving work, and thus he bears the name 'Jesus' or 'Saviour' (Matt. 1:21). Furthermore, he is Lord because of his role in prophecy as Messiah. Therefore he is called 'Christ' (Matt. 16:16, the 'anointed Messiah').

When Paul approaches the end of his prologue to 1 Corinthians, he directs the reader to future events. Again the Lord is central, for in 1 Corinthians 1:7 Paul declares that our Lord Jesus Christ will be revealed. Like us, the first-century Christians had come to believe on the Lord Jesus Christ because of the preached Word. They and we have never seen Jesus in the flesh, but we believe because of the grace of God which convinced us. Some day faith will become redundant, because we shall see him. He will be revealed. God will switch on the light of his deity, and we shall see him. Now, just think about that!

Paul pursues the theme in 1 Corinthians 1:8 when he writes that we will be ready when the 'day of our Lord Jesus Christ' dawns. On that day the Sun of Righteousness will cut through the clouds of human history and we shall be dazzled. Recently we spent a summer week in the Holy Land, and the sun was our main topic of conversation. Its rays were irresistible, its appearance mesmerizing. Some day the Lord will dawn upon human history, and 'every eye will see him' (Rev. 1:7). Just as the Palestinian sun dominated our thinking and speaking, so all other topics of conversation will vanish when the Son of God shines on our world.

There is one final appearance of our word in the prologue to 1 Corinthians. In verse 9 we are told that our Lord is faithful. God called us into fellowship with Jesus Christ. We have come to rely on that experience of his salvation, and just as we live in the light of his lordship, we can also count on all his promises. He is faithful. As the great preacher of another era put it, 'Jesus Christ is a gentleman, and I can count on the word of a gentleman to be true.'

Who's boss?

Meeting a 'real lord' for the first time was for me an unforgettable experience. As a nobility-starved American, I was
quite enchanted. My family and I were touring the motor
museum at Beaulieu in the New Forest. When we came to the
main reception desk, Lord Montagu sat there signing auto-
graphs. Our teenaged daughter quickly thrust her programme
in front of the peer for his signature. I just stood there in awe.

Our biblical word 'lord' has three main uses. The first one
would include Lord Montagu, for the word denotes *important
men*. In the Old Testament we hear Sarah refer to Abraham
as 'my master' (or 'lord') (Gen. 18:12). Here it was a term of
respect applied by the wife to her husband. One still catches
this in German, where the male prefaces his name with *Herr*,
and in Spanish where we have *señor*.

The second use of the word 'lord' in the Bible is the application of 'lord' to *Jesus Christ*. Throughout the New Testament we discover this. Some call him 'Lord' but do not
submit to him, and this deception will be unmasked in the
Day of Judgement (Luke 6:46).

Actually, there is another rather significant appearance of
this word in the New Testament. In Paul's great paean of
praise in Philippians 2:11, we learn that every person who
ever lived on the earth will recognize some day that 'Jesus
Christ is Lord, to the glory of God the Father'. This does not
teach universalism or imply that every person will ultimately
be saved. It does teach that every living being will some day
become aware of the true dominance of the Lord Jesus Christ
in God's plan for this world.

There is also a third use of our word, and this one is in the
Old Testament. *'Jehovah'* is translated in the Old Testament
with 'LORD'. (The capital letters distinguish it from Adonai
which is translated 'Lord'.) John identifies Christ with Jehovah
(John 12:41), referring to Isaiah's vision in the temple (Isa.
6:1-10).

Jehovah LORD is often used in combination with other
names. Here are a few examples. When Abraham went to
offer Isaac on Mount Moriah, the beleaguered believer learned

that Jehovah was the Provider, for the LORD provided a lamb to sacrifice (Gen. 22:14).

When Israel prepared a tabernacle to worship the Lord, Jehovah gave a song of praise to Moses. The name by which the LORD called himself was this: 'I am the LORD, who makes you holy' (Exod. 31:13). He is the Sanctifier of his people, who sets apart sinning and stubborn Israelites to be a holy people.

As Gideon led the children of Israel through the moral roller-coaster during the period of the judges, the LORD encouraged Gideon to know that the LORD is Peace (Judg. 6:24). Here the LORD takes to himself the name 'Shalom' (Peace).

One further use of the combination name is in the Shepherd Psalm, Psalm 23. In the first verse David ascribes to the LORD a combination name. The LORD is Shepherd. Married to the immutable name 'Jehovah' is the role of Shepherd. As true as his eternal character is his pastoral fidelity to his own.

Jews, according to one tradition, were careful not to step on a piece of paper. They picked it up and examined it to make certain that the name of Jehovah, LORD, was not written on it. Would that we as Bible-believing Christians shared that reverence for the name of our Lord.

2.
Cross purposes

'Lest the **cross** *of Christ be emptied of its power'* (1 Cor. 1:17)
'The message of the **cross** *is foolishness to those who are perishing, but to us who are being saved it is the power of God'*
(1 Cor. 1:18)

In Western Europe and North America the cross is almost a 'pop' symbol. It dangles in golden beauty from chains around people's necks. To them it has been reduced to little more than cheap costume jewellery.

For centuries architects have crowned church steeples with a cross. No doubt in times past this was an expression of worship, but now it is only an archaic alternative to a weather-vane.

The cross is also a shorthand symbol for Christianity. One sees this emblem in the banner of the Red Cross. Founded in 1859 by the Swiss Protestant layman, Henri Dunant, the Red Cross attests to its Christian origin by the instantly recognizable insignia. (Interestingly, in Moslem lands the sign is a red crescent.) Few people would today identify the Red Cross with Christianity, but nevertheless the cross continues to be its mark.

Although the cross crops up in many contexts, it is the biblical idea which concerns us. The Greek word for 'cross' is *stauros*, and it occurs twenty-eight times in the New Testament. Only a few technical terms identify this Greek parent with our English language. *Stauro*lite is a mineral comprised of prismic crystals which form themselves in a cross-shape. Also from the field of physics comes the *stauro*scope which is an instrument used to locate planes of light vibration in certain crystals.

Despite the obscurity of English relatives, *stauros* is anything but obscure in New Testament times. In fact, the crux of the divine revelation is the cross. Primarily a Roman device for execution, the cross was found in two forms. Sometimes it was shaped like a capital 'T' with the crossbar at the top. Otherwise it was the shape known to us with the crossbar part way down, as a small 't'.

Hammered together from beams sturdy enough to bear the dead weight of a man, the cross was dragged by the condemned man to a place of execution. He was virtually forced to 'dig his own grave'. Afterwards he was affixed to the cross by either thongs or nails. Finally the cross was raised to an upright position, and the unfortunate victim succumbed by a combination of circulatory failure and broken bones. Sometimes a fire kindled at the foot of the cross suffocated the crucified.

In the Corinthian letter our word 'cross' occurs only twice. Paul asserts that the cross is the sole source of power in proclaiming the gospel. Human wisdom can never comprehend the cross and therefore Paul readily renounced rationalism (1 Cor. 1:17).

This did not imply naivety on Paul's part, for he realized how foolish this message of the cross sounded to sophisticated Greek ears. Only an unconditional commitment to Christ could open one's eyes to see the sense of salvation through the Crucified One (1 Cor. 1:18).

Although the noun 'cross' shows up only twice in 1 Corinthians, the verb 'to crucify' *stauroo* is found in four further texts. In combatting the divisions which sliced through the Corinthian community of believers, Paul holds up the great unifying doctrine, the crucifixion of Christ. He, Paul, was not crucified; Christ was crucified for them (1 Cor. 1:13).

When pressed to compress his gospel into one word, Paul again retreated to the cross. 'We preach Christ crucified,' he asserted. Lest anyone accuse him of oversimplifying, Paul revealed his knowledge that the cross was an offence to the Jews and an enigma to Greeks (1 Cor. 1:23).

It is an insult to say that an apparently intelligent man has a one-track mind, but Paul had. When he entered the arena at Corinth and declared his allegiance to the Lord, he was rigorously single-minded. 'I resolved to know nothing while I was with you except Jesus Christ and him crucified,' Paul offered as a defence for his preaching (1 Cor. 2:2).

The crucifixion of Christ, according to Paul, was a monument to the spiritual blindness of powerful men. Jewish and Roman leaders had failed to grasp the significance of Christ, and thus they slaughtered him. If they had understood, Paul reasoned, 'They would not have crucified the Lord of glory' (1 Cor. 2:8).

In the Corinthian correspondence Paul wrestles with Greek wisdom. Instead of trading logical blows, he reverts continually to the genius of his message: the cross of Christ. The apostle was fully aware of a truth stated later by Spurgeon: 'There are some sciences that may be learned by the head, but the science of Christ crucified can only be learned by the heart.'

Cross roads

It was the American scholar Dr Vernon Grounds who summed up the significance of Calvary for preachers and Bible teachers. 'Pick any text,' Dr Grounds wrote, 'and head straight cross-country to Calvary.'

The entire revelation of God finds its focal point in the cross. From the slaughter of beasts to clothe our first parents to the daily sacrifice in the Jerusalem temple, the primacy of atonement was visible. In the Lamb of God, the Lord Jesus Christ, the entire sacrificial system of the Old Covenant climaxed and concluded.

The cross has three main meanings in New Testament writings. First, it is taken *literally*. In Philippians 2:8 the apostle Paul paints the depth of Christ's condescension with these words: 'He humbled himself and became obedient unto death — even death on a cross.' For the Jew crucifixion was a curse (Deut. 21:23).

In order to humiliate the Jews utterly, the rapacious Roman Titus (A.D.40?-81) caused hundreds to be crucified. In his *Wars of the Jews* Josephus summarized this dastardly deed: 'So the soldiers, out of the wrath and hatred they bore the Jews, nailed those they caught, one after another, to the crosses, by way of jest; when their multitude was so great, that room was wanting for crosses, and crosses wanting for the bodies.'[1]

A second use of the word 'cross' is *symbolical*. Jesus spoke to his disciples when he said, 'Anyone who does not take his cross and follow me is not worthy of me' (Matt. 10:38). A cross is an undeserved burden of health, spirit or relationship. Christians are spurred on to spiritual maturity by bearing such a cross.

Thomas à Kempis (1380-1471), the Spanish Carmelite mystic, underlined the imperative of the cross when he wrote, 'Jesus now has many lovers of his heavenly kingdom, but few bearers of his cross.'

Half a millenium later another Christian mystic wrote in similar vein. A.W. Tozer, the Chicago prophet and penman, expressed the concept of the cross in similar words: 'To be crucified means, first, the man on the cross is facing only one direction; second, he is not going back; and third, he has no further plans of his own.' Complete commitment is the cost of the crucified life of a believer.

A final application of the cross is central to the New Testament. This is specifically the *cross of Christ*. To the Galatians Paul explained the opposition which his ministry aroused. It was solely attributable to the 'offence of the cross' (Gal. 5:11). By the same token the only solution to a polarized world is the cross of Christ. In the cosmopolitan city of Ephesus many ethnic and racial groups were represented. All of these could be reconciled to one another only by being reconciled to God through the cross of Christ (Eph. 2:16).

Christ crucified is the genius of the gospel. 'God was reconciling the world to himself in Christ, not counting men's sins against them' (2 Cor. 5:19). 'He himself bore our sins in his body on the tree' (1 Peter 2:24). Most other world religions make much of their founder's teaching or even his deeds. Christianity alone makes the death of its Founder to be the glory of his followers. In the seventeenth century the French Jesuit, Louis Bourdaloue (1632-1704), 'king of the orators and orator of kings', caught the secret of Christ's cross in this unforgettable statement: 'In the cross of Christ excess in men

is met by excess in God; excess of evil is mastered by excess
of love.'

1. Josephus, *Wars of the Jews*, Book V, ch. XI.

3.
God's foolishness

'Foolishness *to those who are perishing'* (1 Cor. 1:18)

'Fools rush in where angels fear to tread,' wrote Alexander Pope (1688-1744) in his *Essay on Criticism*. Pope was mainly interested in literature, but his principle can be applied to many situations.

Following the same line of reasoning, John Lyly (1554-1606) added, 'There's no fool like an old fool.' Of course, the common denominator between Pope and Lyly is the little word 'fool'. It creates a uniformly negative impression, whether we meet the fool in literature or life.

It is the Bible which turns the term 'fool' in a positive direction. In 1 Corinthians 1:18 the apostle Paul asserts that unconverted people cannot grasp the gospel by themselves. In fact, 'the message of the cross is foolishness to those who are perishing'. One thinks of preachers on street corners in big cities who endure the sneers of passers-by. The suave sophisticates find such preaching to be utter folly. That is the reason why most Christians are too cowardly to do it.

God has reduced man's common sense to utter foolishness (1 Cor. 1:20). His method of demolishing the colossus of Greek wisdom was nothing else but the foolishness of preaching! (1 Cor. 1:21.) The world looks on preaching as foolishness, because biblical proclamation flies in the face of human wisdom.

One recalls Jesus' story about the gentleman farmer, a real modern manager. He tore down old barns, hastily erecting new ones. Crops were then crammed into the new storage facilities. When the farmer finally took time to think, it was too late. For the call of God broke into his smug reverie. 'You fool!' God deflated him, 'This very night your life will be demanded from you' (Luke 12:20).

The very idea of a messianic hero being nailed up on a

cross defied the comprehension of Greek philosophers (1 Cor. 1:23). How could such an obviously God-blessed being be slain by wicked men? Could or should not he have struck down his executioners? In complete disbelief Napoleon expressed this. Classifying himself with Caesar and Charlemagne, Napoleon said all of these had built their empires on force. By contrast Christ had built his on love, and millions had suffered martyrdom for Christ and his kingdom.

Paul reasoned in 1 Corinthians that 'the foolishness of God is wiser than man's wisdom' (1 Cor. 1:25). Here is a comparison which is ludicrous. To compare God's wisdom with man's is like placing a mud puddle alongside the Atlantic. Their only similarity is wetness. So when God's wisdom and man's are seen together, the ideas are simply incomparable. Man's attempts to discern God's wisdom are like a goldfish lecturing on calculus.

Not only does God's wisdom look foolish to man's puny mind, God's agents also arouse accusations of foolishness. He has chosen few of the wise, witty or well-born. His choice appears to be foolish (1 Cor. 1:26-28). Still the world was transformed by these mundane ministers. The church father Origen (about 185-254) answered this criticism in his essay against Celsus, who castigated Christians as 'foolish and low individuals, and persons devoid of perception, and slaves, and women, and children'.[1]

No doubt the first chapter of 1 Corinthians is Paul's inspired defence of God's sovereignty, and it simply shatters our narrow, man-made ideas. So sin-struck is man that he cannot even grasp God's gospel on his own. To put it in Paul's words, 'Man without the Spirit does not accept the things that come from the Spirit of God, for they are foolishness to him' (1 Cor. 2:14).

This explains why apparently clever folk fail to figure out faith. Only the grace of God can lift the covers from the redemptive truth. In order to attain spiritual wisdom one must become a fool by human standards (1 Cor. 3:17-18).

Paul put his finger on the subject of foolishness by personal identification. 'We are fools for Christ,' Paul admitted (1 Cor. 4:10). He had believed a message which was folly to

the fancy of Greek ears. His involvement in preaching the
message of Christ drew Paul into further foolishness, according to the Greeks. The Corinthian Christians did not simply
laugh off the matter, they reacted with acute embarrassment.
Undeterred, Paul persisted in believing and declaring the
Christian gospel.

The Greek words translated 'foolish' are *moria* and *moros*.
One can easily guess the nearest English relative, 'moron'. A
moron is a very stupid person who is unable to cover up his
limitations. What a comparison this is for Christians, who
appear to the world as either moderately or completely
stupid! Really, they are walking in the wisdom of God, and
someday God will prove it to the whole world.

Suffering fools gladly

According to a modern motto, an intelligent man 'does not
suffer fools gladly'. In other words, let someone make a stupid
remark, and this person cuts the foolish conversationalist
down to size. Few people realize that this phrase comes from
2 Corinthians 11:19. The apostle Paul tells the Corinthians to
look upon him as a fool, if they cannot see spiritual wisdom
in his work and words.

Our word *moria* or *moron* (foolish) is applied in two ways
by biblical writers. First, it refers to *people*. In his Sermon on
the Mount, Jesus called one man a fool. He was the person
who built his house on the sand, and he was a word picture
of the fool who fails to found his life upon the Word of God
(Matt. 7:26). According to the Lord, anyone who tries to
build a life apart from the Bible is a fool. One thinks of a
phenomenally wealthy man like John Paul Getty, the oil
magnate. He built his life upon wise investment of time and
money, but he failed to invest in eternity. At the end he confessed to having never known either true friendship or real
love.

In Matthew 25:2-8 the Lord introduces a company of
foolish people. They are those who fail to prepare for the
coming of Christ, like wedding guests who neglect to buy fuel

for their little oriental lamps until it is too late and the bride-groom has entered.

A fool is one who plays the ostrich by plunging his head into the sand to avoid seeing what is unpleasant. Everyone has heard of the person who senses that he is a 'bit off colour'. Little lumps appear on his body, and ominously they grow. Still the person pretends the symptoms are not there. When it is too late he turns to a physician who diagnoses terminal cancer. This foolish procrastination costs the victim his life.

The New Testament uses our word in a second sense when it is applied to *speech*. 'Foolish and stupid arguments . . . produce quarrels' in the church of Jesus Christ (2 Tim. 2:23). Under the guise of an upright search for truth, many people devote their energies to introducing subjects into church meetings which are guaranteed to arouse argument. These inevitably acrimonious discussions always yield more heat than light. The only winner is the fool who started the scrap, because he becomes famous, indeed infamous. The church of Jesus Christ is the loser.

In writing to his assistant Titus, Paul instructs him to 'avoid foolish controversies and genealogies and arguments and quarrels about the law' (Titus 3:9). Now obviously such debates display one's knowledge of religious facts, but the value of knowing these facts is extremely questionable. One recalls a gifted colleague on a Bible college faculty, who delighted in turning every faculty meeting into a game of one-upmanship. Ten years later he is a miserable man, although he never lost an argument.

The church of Christ has always had its share of fools who majored on minus issues. They may have mastered all the facts of religion, but they missed the meaning. As the church marched triumphantly through human history, they crouched along the way mumbling about issues of eternal insignificance. The title they earned is that of being fools in the eyes of God and man.

1. Origen, *Contra Celsus*

4.
Testimonial match

Driving through the rain-slick streets of a German city some years ago, I suffered a minor collision with another car. The lady's wing was wrinkled, and a policeman quickly arrived on the scene. When it came to reporting the accident, my passenger was asked for a statement. To my dismay, my friend saw the accident as my fault. He gave a true, although damaging, testimony.

Our term 'testimony' has remarkable similarities with English, for the Greek word is *marturion*. From it comes our word 'martyr', one who dies for a cause. Actually, martyrdom is carrying testimony to the extreme. By the end of the apostolic age martyrdom was equated with death (Acts 22:20).

In 1 Corinthians 2:1 the testimony of Paul points Godward. He was not sociological in his pronouncements, and he did not aim at changing society by radical reform. Neither was he philosophical, attempting to move men to think better thoughts. Of course, he was not political; he never debated the question of Roman rule versus Jewish sovereignty. Paul kept close to God in all his writing and speaking.

A second occurrence of 'testimony' is in 1 Corinthians 1:6. The apostolic declaration of divine power was confirmed in the experience of the hearers. Only by commitment can spiritual truth be discerned. By way of illustration, one thinks of a mango. A mango by definition is an 'oblong, yellowish-red tropical fruit'. That covers the matter remarkably well, but it gives no idea of taste. To savour the sweetness of a mango, one must bite into the juicy meat and simply enjoy it. By the same token, one can only comprehend Christ's grace by personal experience of repentance and faith.

A third appearance of the word 'testimony' is found in 1 Corinthians 15:15. There Paul sets himself up as a 'witness' (literally 'testifier') who testified to the resurrection of Christ. Paul had the same qualifications as we do to testify to the risen Redeemer. He had been apprehended by the Lord on the Damascus Road and we, too, can testify to such a meeting on life's road.

When we progress to Paul's other Corinthian letter, our word is also found there. A clear conscience testifies to the sanctifying work of the Holy Spirit (2 Cor. 1:12). One of the inestimable benefits of believing on Christ is being at peace with oneself. Paul obviously revelled in this.

In using the Macedonian Christians as an example of generosity, Paul said, 'I *testify* that they gave as much as they were able, and even beyond their ability' (2 Cor. 8:3). In our city there is a large Anglican congregation which excels in missionary giving, and this is known throughout the city and the country. What a marvellous claim to fame is Christian generosity!

One final use of our word is found in 2 Corinthians 13:1, where Paul promises to visit the Corinthians, so that his testimony may add weight to the teaching they have received. How we as Christians should support one another by our individual testimonies! These then have a cumulative effect which greatly enhances the credibility of the Christian message.

Nothing but the truth

At one time there was a Christian musical group on the south coast of England known as 'Nothing but the truth'. It was a cumbersome label, but it was applicable. Two members of the band were lawyers. For some reason, they never warmed to my alternative name, 'the singing solicitors'! They had a firm commitment to communicate God's truth.

Our word 'testimony' has four major uses in the New Testament. First, it *attests to facts*. Jesus confounded Nicodemus by claiming to give accurate testimony concerning the rebirth (John 3:11). In the midst of Samaria's spiritual chaos, the voice of a woman was raised in testimony: 'Many of the Samaritans . . . believed in him because of the woman's testi-

mony' (John 4:39). Christ testified a good confession before
Pilate (1 Tim. 6:13). In each case they attested to facts of
spiritual significance.

J.C. Macaulay, the saintly Scottish preacher who has served
for many years in America and Canada, summarizes the
discipline of personal testimony: 'So long as our personal
testimony exalts the glory and all-sufficiency of Christ as
Saviour, rather than our character either before or after conversion, it will be helpful.' Christian testimony must focus on
the Lord alone, not our emotional experience.

A second aspect of the testimony is seen in *praise for a
person*. Hebrews chapter 11 has been called the 'Westminster
Abbey of Faith'. It includes this commendation as part of the
introduction: faith is 'what the ancients were commended for'
('testified to') (Heb. 11:2). Note how difficult this is to
express in the English language. A godly woman is 'well known
for' ('testified of') 'her good deeds' (1 Tim. 5:10). Here we
have biblical character witnesses. It is commendable to be
'mentioned in despatches' during wartime, but being praised
by biblical testimony must be the epitome. No human praise,
no matter how eminent, can compare with this.

There is a third and negative use of the word in *false testimony*. The fact that it was forbidden in the Ten Commandments never eradicated the practice. When the Jewish
ecclesiastical establishment set about prosecuting the Lord,
they found no evidence against him. Therefore, they fabricated false testimony against him, 'but their statements did not
agree' (Mark 14:56). Stephen, the sterling follower of the
Lord, was likewise the victim of a 'dirty tricks' scheme (Acts
6:12-14).

Christians of every age have felt the sting of false accusa-
tion. Even Charles Haddon Spurgeon's son, Thomas, was
assailed by false witnesses. Thomas was preaching in Australia
when a malicious morsel filtered back to Britain and almost
broke his ailing father's heart.[1]

Predictably the fourth use of our word is *martyrdom*, being put to death for the faith. As indicated earlier, Stephen was declared by the apostle Paul to be a martyr (Acts 22:20). In the book of Revelation there is a cryptic mention of Antipas, God's faithful martyr, who was slain at Pergamum (Rev. 2:13). On a larger scale there is the mention of myriads of martyrs, whose blood bears witness to the Lord Jesus Christ (Rev. 17:6). In each case the word 'martyr' is *marturion*.

Since my birth millions have been martyred by governments of diverse stripes. The Nazi régime in Germany slew not only Jews, but also thousands of Christian pastors and laymen. The Soviets and their satellites have likewise squeezed the life out of a glorious band of believers. In Africa the name of Idi Amin drips with the blood of the saints. One could also speak of China, Chile and Czechoslovakia. Martyrdom is foreign to comfortable Westerners, but it is a fact of life (and death) to thousands of our brothers and sisters. Surely this is the ultimate testimony.

1. Warren Wiersbe, *Listening to the Giants*, p.124.

5.
Mind transplant

'Who has known the **mind** *of the Lord?'* (1 Cor. 2:16)
'We have the **mind** *of Christ'* (1 Cor. 2:16)

Ours is a day of highly technical and reasonably successful transplant surgery. It is almost routine to remove an offensive hip joint and insert an artificial one. Recently a member of our church underwent temporary knee repair with a view to later replacement, when techniques had become more advanced.

This says nothing of the frequent transplants of organs. Nearby we have a major centre for kidney transplants. The matching of tissue now ensures that most transplants are successful. Similar procedures trade defective corneas for good ones, insert healthy bone marrow to offset degeneration and replace faulty hearts with sound ones.

The Bible speaks of a spiritual transplant, by which the mind of Christ is implanted in spiritually dead human beings. It is the word 'mind' which we here consider. The Greek noun is *nous*. Its English namesakes are normally found in the field of philosophy. For instance, 'nous' stands for reason, and God is seen as the 'World Reason' by some philosophers. Immanuel Kant defined the object of rational observance as *'nou*men'.

In 1 Corinthians 2:16 our word shows up twice. The first is a quotation from Isaiah 40:13: 'Who has understood the Spirit' (or 'mind') of the Lord?' The point is this: God operates on a completely different wavelength from us. His mind is unencumbered by human limitations: he is infinite. This renders God's thought processes as impenetrable to men as a man's thoughts are to a goldfish. By unaided rational research we can never grasp God's purposes.

In the second half of 1 Corinthians 2:16 the answer to our powerlessness is stated: 'We have the *mind* of Christ.' God has given his children the very mind of Christ, so that they can take in spiritual truth. The amazing aspect is this: that the most simple soul controlled by the Master's mind takes in and gives out mind-boggling spiritual truth. Meanwhile the most brilliant worldling fails to fathom it.

Our possession of Christ's mind moulds us together in a fellowship of the like-minded. According to 1 Corinthians 1:10, Christians should be 'perfectly united in *mind* and thought'. This is no superficial 'goose-step' thinking which produces Christians who are intellectual clones of a commanding pastor or layman. It is rather such a depth of commitment to Christ that many human differences disappear in our unity.

When the apostle Paul turns to the role of the Holy Spirit in this likeminded fellowship, he uses the word 'mind' to mean understanding. According to the apostle, we should worship intelligently. Those who pray in another tongue pray without understanding: the 'mind is unfruitful' (1 Cor. 14:14). In the opinion of Paul, it is better to both pray and sing with the mind (1 Cor. 14:15).

This has really revolutionary implications for contemporary 'charismatic renewal' fellowships. When one worships, the mind should not be placed in neutral gear. Christians are not merely mechanical chorus machines, which run on with endless repeats of choruses totally oblivious to the meaning of worship. They bring their God-controlled brains to bear on their praise. It is the mind of Christ which masters their worship.

Master's mind

Our world is full of little re*mind*ers. 'Mind the step' directs our attention to a dangerously irregular step. 'Mind how you go' is a good general warning which fits every situation, from the teenager at the wheel of your car to the elderly relative with navigational difficulties. One even warns a talkative friend, 'Mind your tongue,' lest you end up with egg on your face and your foot in your mouth. (That's no mere mixed metaphor, it's a total hash!)

'Mind' in the New Testament has several meanings. First, it refers to *understanding*. When Jesus met the disciples on the Emmaus road, he 'opened their *minds* so that they could understand the Scriptures' (Luke 24:45). Under Holy Spirit inspiration, Paul passed on the helpful truth that 'the peace of God which transcends all understanding, will guard your hearts and your *minds* in Christ Jesus' (Phil. 4:7). In both cases 'mind' and 'understanding' are used as synonyms.

The Roman philosopher and political advisor Seneca (4 B.C.-A.D.65) enunciated a practical principle of survival in the hurly-burly of late Roman civilization: 'Let us train our minds to desire what the situation demands.' In a real sense, only God, who knows all, can prepare our minds to cope with every challenge.

Another application of the mind to understanding is seen in the writings of William Lyon Phelps (1865-1943), the American educator, who devoted his life to training the mind. He warned that at a 'certain age some people's minds close up; they live on their intellectual fat'. How true this is of many evangelical Christians, who have long since stopped serious study of either the Scriptures or of books other than that spiritual 'porn' which panders to nothing but emotional experience!

A second application of the word 'mind' is *intellect*, man's invisible part in contrast to the body. The apostle Paul finds this to be the battleground of sanctification. In Romans he finds a force at work against the 'law of my *mind*', which takes him captive to the law of sin (Rom. 7:23). With his mind he knows what is right, but his body is still responsive to the tyranny of temptation. He is being torn apart: 'I myself in my *mind* am a slave to God's law, but in the sinful nature a slave to the law of sin' (Rom. 7:25). No Christian who is honest with himself can deny that this tension is a terrible fact of life. One lives in the cross-fire between mind and the sinful nature.

John Milton (1608-74), the writer of magnificent masterpieces, showed spiritual sensitivity in *Paradise Lost*. 'The mind is its own place', Milton postulated, 'and in itself can make a Heaven of Hell, a Hell of Heaven.'[1] Here he stated in literary style a truth which permeates the apostolic writings.

One final meaning of the word 'mind' should be considered. This is the *attitude of mind*, a way of thinking. In Romans 12:2 the Christian is urged to lay aside the world's attitudes and allow the Spirit to infuse a godly viewpoint. In writing to the Ephesian church, Paul urged them likewise to be 'made new in the attitude of your *minds*' (Eph. 4:23). A word of warning to the Colossians deters them from the 'unspiritual *mind*' which puffs up a person with idle notions (Col. 2:18). Some Christians are poisoned by 'depraved *minds*' (2 Tim. 3:8).

Human attitudes tend to become entrenched. It is far easier to deceive oneself than it is to change one's mind. In fact, this is the great deterrent to growth among most Christian individuals and fellowships. Approaching the problem from a secular side, the economist Professor John Kenneth Galbraith stated it simply. 'Faced with the choice between changing one's mind and proving there is no need to do so,' Galbraith quipped, 'almost everyone gets busy on the proof.' How often do Christians listen to the exposition of the Bible, nod approvingly and then continue on in the same religious rut!

God made our minds as surely as he fabricated our bodies. Therefore the right employment of our mental facilities is the discernment of his truth, an insight which is Spirit-induced and available only to regenerate reason. It was Johannes Kepler (1571-1630), the German astronomer, who summarized this principle of knowing. In his researches, Kepler declared, he was 'thinking God's thoughts after him'.

1. John Milton, *Paradise Lost*, book 1, line 254.

6.
Flesh and blood

'Men of the **flesh***'* (1 Cor. 3:1, RSV)
'You are still of the **flesh***'* (1 Cor. 3:3, RSV)
'Are you not of the **flesh***?'* (1 Cor. 3:3, RSV)

'Blood is thicker than water,' means that family relationships usually take precedence over other social connections. 'After all,' reasons the normal person, 'he is my own flesh and blood.' There is a feeling of fraternity which arises instantly between blood relatives.

Some years ago we were driving through a small town near Chicago, when I noticed a flashing sign: 'Detzler Car Sales'. Immediately I stopped, but my pessimism asserted itself. 'It *can't* be Detzler. There are too few of us in America.' Later investigations revealed a distant relationship. In fact, I learned there are ninety-nine families of Detzlers in America.

It is the influence of flesh and blood which Paul asserts in 1 Corinthians 3:1-3, His emphasis is negative, because the Corinthian Christians have been allowing themselves to be dominated by their fleshly impulses rather than those of the Holy Spirit.

The word which is translated 'fleshly' in the RSV is rendered 'carnal' in the AV and 'worldly' in the NIV. To focus our attention more clearly, therefore, we consider the Greek word, *sarkikos* or *sarkinos* ('fleshly'), the adjective version of *sarks* (body or flesh). We see this revealed in such a word as '*sarco*phagus'. Originally 'sarcophagus' meant literally 'body-eater', because coffins were carved out of limestone to speed the disintegration of the body. Now it means any stone coffin.

Let's leave this macabre subject and turn to biblical considerations. Our word occurs three times in 1 Corinthians 3:1-3. According to verse 1, 'men of the flesh' are 'babes in Christ' (RSV). The tell-tale sign of such spiritual infancy is resistance to Bible truth, and most pastors have a nursery full of spiritual 'bottle babies'. Go beyond a simple gospel message, and they simply nod off or move off.

In 1 Corinthians 3:3 we find that these spiritually spoiled children are not only bottle babies, they are also cry babies. They raise a dreadful din whenever they fail to get their way in the church. Around them hovers a dark cloud of 'jealousy and strife'. As they sit in church their faces look as though they would turn apple juice to vinegar at a glance. Initiate conversation, and they unleash a tirade.

Later on in 1 Corinthians 9:11 Paul uses our word in a positive way. Here he refers to the 'material' *(sarkika)* 'benefits' which should accrue to the preachers of the gospel. They should derive physical support in exchange for the spiritual ministry they give.

When he wrote again to the Corinthians Paul employed our word to distinguish his message from human fabrications. The apostolic ministry was marked not by 'worldly wisdom' (NIV) or 'fleshly wisdom' (AV) (2 Cor. 1:12). Paul denies that worldly means can achieve spiritual ends. A modern advocate of this principle was A.W. Tozer (1897-1963), who wrote, 'I think the church *has* failed, not by neglecting to provide leadership but by living too much like the world . . . The world wants the church to add a dainty spiritual touch to its carnal schemes, and to be there to help it to its feet and put it to bed when it comes home drunk with fleshly pleasures.'[1]

Again in 2 Corinthians 10:4 Paul decries the reliance on 'the weapons of the world' to fight spiritual foes. The AV shows the true pedigree of this word when it translates this verse: 'For the weapons of our warfare are not carnal, but mighty through God to the pulling down of strongholds.'

It appears that Christians often arm themselves with worldly weapons, and then wonder why they lose spiritual battles. 'If we can put on a little play, perhaps the Bible will be more relevant.' Our music is propelled by as much electronic wattage as money can buy, but in the process we sacrifice spiritual power. We even try to persuade people by clever argument and illustrated lecture that creation is true, but they have never met the Creator. They laugh at our puny attempts to fight spiritual warfare with intellectual implements. It is like trying to extinguish a tanker fire with a water pistol.

Again we turn to Tozer who put it so cogently in *The Divine Conquest*: 'When the Church joins up with the world it is the true Church no longer but only a pitiful hybrid thing, an object of smiling contempt to the world and an abomination to the Lord.'[2]

Tomb of the soul

Plato (427?-347 B.C.), the Greek philosopher, had a hearty mistrust of the flesh, *sarks*. To him the 'flesh was the tomb of the soul'. This is the 'caged eagle' theory of human life. Our superior spirit is caged in the inferior body. Only when the cage is sprung by death can the soul fly free.

Christians consider this view to be blasphemy. It makes material things intrinsically evil. Since God moulded man in his hand and breathed into him a living spirit, God must be the author of evil. That view just does not agree with Genesis 1:31, which insists that everything God made was good. It was Satan slithering into the garden who introduced sin. The body was no more evil than the spirit, and the spirit was not morally superior to the body.

Our word *sarkikos* ('fleshly') has two basic meanings in the New Testament. The first refers to all that is *natural*. When writing to Roman Christians Paul urged them to 'share with them [Palestinian Jews] their *material* blessings' (Rom. 15:27). As expected, famine had descended upon Palestine, and Paul canvassed Christians from Rome to Syria, collecting aid for their endangered brethren. (This casts some brilliant light on the apostolic social conscience.) 'Material' ('fleshly') things were seen as fodder for Christian charity. How often we write off possessions as being dirty, especially when someone else possesses them! Paul saw them as vehicles of blessing.

Another positive use of our word is in Hebrews 7:16. There the author portrays the priesthood of Christ. His office rested not upon his 'ancestry' (his physical descendance from Aaron) but upon 'the power of an indestructible life'. In God's economy the Lord Jesus Christ officiated as the High Priest, not by being Aaron's flesh and blood, but by deriving his life from the Father, God himself.

There is, however, a second use of our word in the New Testament, and this one is negative. In fact, it is downright *nasty*. In 1 Peter 2:11 the Christian is warned to 'abstain from *sinful*' ('fleshly') 'desires, which war against your soul'. The flesh is part of that predatory trinity: world, flesh and devil.

In Romans 7:14, Paul portrays the Christian's conflict. 'We know that the law is spiritual,' he concedes, 'but I am *unspiritual*' (literally 'fleshly'), 'sold as a slave to sin.' This contrast Paul presses throughout Romans 7, until both the comparison and the apostle are exhausted like a squeezed lemon. My human nature is locked in life or death conflict with my spiritual being, but this conflict is only distressing to a Christian who longs to live the life God meant him to have.

Jesus himself referred to the secret of triumph over these destructive drives. When explaining the facts of new life to Nicodemus, Jesus said, '*Flesh* gives birth to *flesh*, but the Spirit gives birth to spirit' (John 3:6). Unless true spiritual life is present, one has no hope of triumphing over the sinful desires of one's body.

That lesser light of Puritanism, George Swinnock, summarized Christian combat succinctly: 'The world is therefore a purgatory,' (he rejected the Catholic view) 'that it might not be our paradise.' When the battle with our sinful nature becomes heated and threatening, we remember that God has already told us the outcome: unqualified victory.

1. A.W. Tozer, *Man: The Dwelling Place of God*, pp.138-9.
2. A.W. Tozer, *The Divine Conquest*, p.110.

7.
Master Builder

'Someone else is **building** *on it'* (1 Cor. 3:10)
'One should be careful how he **builds**' (1 Cor. 3:10)
'If any man **builds** *on this foundation'* (1 Cor. 3:12)

Building is a demanding business. Some years ago I was teaching in a small Bible college. Growth in enrolment forced us to erect a student residence. Once the decision was made, the principal contacted an architect (same word as Paul's 'master builder', Greek *architekton*). The architect turned all his talents to planning, persuading the local authorities, and then pushing the builders. It was a long, tedious business, but the college now occupies one of the very few purpose-built facilities.

It is the idea of 'building' that we now consider. The Greek word is *epoikodomeo* ('I build upon'). Three words are married to supply this term. One is the prefix *epi* (upon). A second prefix is *oiko*, as seen in *eco*nomics (literally, 'home laws', managing the home).

In our compound Greek term the second half is the word *doma* ('roof'). This root is found in such English words as 'domestic' (at school domestic science teaches skills useful at home) or 'domicile' (a place of residence). Together our Greek word means literally 'to build a roof'. The emphasis is on building a dwelling-place.

In 1 Corinthians 3:10 the word occurs twice. By God's grace Paul (the 'architect') has laid a solid foundation, the Lord Jesus Christ. Others are even now building on it. It is the apostolic warning that those others should 'be careful how they build'. Building is serious business. When one lays a row of bricks which are not level, the wall ultimately stands crooked. This is the danger in spiritual building, too. Insert one false teaching, and the entire house of God leans to one side.

Not only must one build straight, but one must also take care to use the right materials. In 1 Corinthians 3:12 we find the instruction to 'build on the foundation using gold, silver, costly stones'. This is coupled with a strong warning not to build with 'wood, hay or straw'. Building materials must suit the foundation and the climate. For instance, an ice igloo is suitable for the North Pole, but on the equator it would be a diminishing asset. The material is not suited to either the foundation or the climate.

One further occurrence of our word is found in 1 Corinthians 3:14. Here the apostle Paul looks to the purpose of his building. 'If what he has built survives,' Paul says of the builder in Christ's kingdom, 'he will receive his reward.' Christians are building for the future.

When we lived in Germany many people began to build houses. They did not have enough money to complete them, but they made a start. The second generation took up the task, and both families lived together. It was a family home in the largest sense of the word. Grandparents had invested time and savings to build for future generations. Christians, too, are building for the future.

We may not see the whole building completed; in fact, we shall only see a small part finished. Our little contribution shrinks when we compare it to what has gone before. Generations of faithful labourers have worked on the erection of God's church. Should the Lord prolong human history, many more generations will build after us. Ours is the task of building straight, using sound materials and according to a standard which God has set.

Build to last

During times of economic retrenchment, one of the main signs of depression is the decline in so-called 'building-starts'. How many houses are begun in any given year? How many flats are started? What building work is undertaken in any given year? In boom times people rush to put money into bricks and mortar. When money is short, there is little left for investment in such construction.

Our Greek word is used in both literal and figurative ways. *Literally* it means to build, and the simple form *(oikodomeo)* was taken by Jesus to describe the man who set about to build a tower (Luke 14:28). This simple and rather common undertaking was used by Jesus to teach the cost of commitment. Anyone who starts to build counts the cost. Likewise one who essays to follow Jesus must count the cost. Otherwise he will leave an unfinished building because his resources are exhausted. How many people have left unfinished lives of discipleship? (Luke 14:29-30.)

The more common use of our word in the New Testament is *spiritual*, to build disciples up in the Lord. The abovementioned Bible college many years ago adopted the unofficial motto: 'Building people'. Surely this is a laudable aim for a Bible college. It is also the main task of every local church: to build people up in the faith so they can go out with the gospel.

Paul was particularly enamoured of this idea. To the Ephesians he wrote that the church was 'built on the foundation of the apostles and prophets, with Christ Jesus himself as the chief corner-stone' (Eph. 2:20). Christians who come adrift from the biblical foundation are also separated from the Lord. In the New Testament there is no such thing as a mystical attachment to Christ which shuns a spiritual reliance on the Scriptures.

When writing to the Colossians, Paul again turned to this idea of building. He reminded them that they had been 'rooted and built up' in Christ (Col. 2:7). Here the emphasis falls on stability. Too often spiritual stability is caricatured as being dead traditionalism. Nothing could be further from the truth, because he, Paul, points to that spiritual strength which is unbent by the wind of adversity and the floods of trouble.

A final reference to our relatively uncommon form, *epoikodomeo* ('to build upon'), is found in the little letter of Jude. There that servant of Christ and brother of James (v.1) urges his readers: 'Build yourselves up in your most holy faith and pray in the Holy Spirit' (v.20). Christian character is not a 'portacabin', which is dropped into our garden all finished the moment we are saved. No, Christian character takes a lot of building. According to Jude, the signs of spiritual growth are two. First, faith expands. As a Christian I can trust God for more this year than I could last year. And the second sign is prayer in the Holy Spirit. My prayer life should become increasingly spiritual and decreasingly material. The longer God builds me up, the more my gaze will be deflected from the gifts and riveted on the Giver. This is being built up in the faith.

Is your life a building rising as a temple to the Holy Spirit, or is it still a shack, cobbled together from bits of tin and cardboard?

8.
Judge for yourself

'I care very little if I am **judged** *by you or by any human court;
indeed, I do not even* **judge** *myself'* (1 Cor. 4:3)
'It is the Lord who **judges** *me'* (1 Cor. 4:4)
'Judge *nothing before the appointed time'* (1 Cor. 4:5)

Critics in the newspaper are bad enough. Often I enjoy a
television programme until I read the reviews the next morning. Immediately the perspicacious word-smith destroys my
pleasure and informs me that the whole presentation was
below my intellectual standards. But I *thought* I liked it.

Criticism can have a positive aspect, however. Many great
preachers of the Word have been critics of contemporary
society. God has used them to deliver a divine perspective
through the preaching of his Word.

The critical faculty of discernment is the emphasis of
1 Corinthians 4:1-7. Our word 'judgement' arises from the
Greek words *krisis* ('judgement') or *kriterion* ('judgement') or
krites ('judge'). The connection to 'critic', 'criterion' and
'crisis' (a decisive experience) is clearly seen.

Our passage from 1 Corinthians 4 contains two combination
words. In verses 3-4 we have the Greek word *anakrinō* ('to
examine'). Judgement by human beings is unreliable, because
it is fickle and futile. The Christian worker cannot be sensitive
to every critic, or he will be paralysed and unable to do anything. This invalidity of human judgement extends to self-
judgement. My view of myself and my ministry is often
coloured either by unwarranted optimism or unrealistic
pessimism. Surely human judgement is an unreliable indicator
of spiritual impact (1 Cor. 4:3).

Many Christian workers simply give up because of carping
criticism. They cannot please all the people all the time, and
they fear they are not pleasing any of the people any of the
time. In reality they should be striving to please God alone.

In my experience the Christian ministry is strewn with the carcases of Christian workers shot down by critics. They have silenced the nightingale, but no one reproduces the song.

In 1 Corinthians 4:5 Paul warns Christians to suspend judgement: 'Judge nothing before the appointed time.' How often do we seek to assess spiritual results before they are revealed by God! The only exercise some Christians ever have is jumping to conclusions.

There are three reasons at least why we should not judge prematurely. First, we are limited in our experience. We may never have encountered that situation before. Second, we are restricted in our understanding. We cannot possibly plumb the depths of human motivation. We just do not know why our brother or sister has acted as he or she has. Third, our judgement is coloured by our wishes. We know what we would like to see happen, and we often let this determine our assessment of any given person or work.

There is a second combination word which includes 'judgement'. In 1 Corinthians 4:7 the NIV puts it this way: 'Who *makes you different*' ('judges between', *diakrono*) 'from anyone else?' The word here means to distinguish, to make a difference. God is the source of diversity in our world. England is a pluralistic society with people from the Commonwealth and beyond. Furthermore, there is an evident difference between people in our society. One cannot simply sweep natural differences under the carpet. In our church there are gifted musicians and tone-deaf people, and 'The Lord God made them all'. He distinguishes between people, so let us not deny these distinctions and by implication undo God's work.

Make your mind up

Life is really a chain of decisions. We make big decisions such as those on career, marriage and place of residence. Of course, our commitment to Christ determines all other decisions. (Woe to the man or woman who wilfully puts things above God, and thus sells his soul!)

It is this decision-making which flavours the words we are considering. The basic word *krinō*, 'judge', entails decision. In Acts 16:15 Lydia asks the apostles to decide whether or not she displays spiritual life. (This is a decision we all face in Christian work.)

The Lord Jesus Christ uses this word. In John 5:30 he claims that his 'judgement is just'. He will pronounce unbiased and completely informed judgement on the human race. This is a comfort to the 'justified', but a terror to the unjust.

Paul presents the human inability to judge in Romans 2:1: 'You, therefore, have no excuse, you who pass judgement on someone else, for at whatever point you judge the other, you are condemning yourself, because you who pass judgement do the same things.' What insight into human life is expressed in that sentence! People are always trying to cover up their own sins by the condemnation of others.

The German poet and dramatist Johann Christoph Friedrich von Schiller (1759-1805) said, 'World history is world judgement.' He thought all judgement took place within history, but he was wrong. God will judge evil in eternity, and this is the only comfort to downtrodden people.

Our second word, *anakrinō* ('to examine') is also a frequent participant in biblical vocabulary. Paul praised the Berean Christians because they '*examined* the Scriptures every day to see if what Paul said was true' (Acts 17:11).

Christians today could learn a thing or two from the Bereans. Most modern believers settle for instant spirituality. They read a few Bible study notes, which pre-digest the text. Never do they engage in serious study of the Bible itself. Instead of spiritual nourishment, they settle for a sort of Christian pep-pill. Consequently they soon suffer from malnutrition. This is especially true of the hurried businessman who dashes into the presence of the Lord and retreats unblessed day after day.

Our final word is *diakronō* ('to distinguish'). God 'made no distinction' between Jews and Gentiles, for 'he purified their hearts by faith' (Acts 15:9).

People are urged to exercise spiritual discernment. Jesus told the disciples: 'You know how to *interpret*' (*diakrinō*) 'the appearance of the sky, but you cannot interpret the signs of the times' (Matt. 16:3).

Diversity and difference are marks of God's creativity in our world. He makes nature so rich in variety and fits a rainbow array of people into it. The church of Jesus Christ likewise reflects this marvellous diversity. Different nations with their varied traditions and cultures combine in our churches. Many gifts are necessary to fill out the ministry of the church, and this diversity is also a gift of God to us. Praise the Lord he made us different!

9.
Father's day

'In Christ Jesus I became your **father** *through the gospel'*
(1 Cor. 4:15)

The day I became a father is etched indelibly on my memory. Actually, it was a night, a frigid winter's night near Chicago. The roads resembled skating rinks. We had driven carefully to the hospital, about fifteen miles from home. In the early morning hours the doctor came to the waiting room and awakened me with these words: 'Wayne, you have a daughter.'

It was my final year of theological studies, and we possessed very little. Our flat was small and cramped. Income was derived from part-time work for a professor and as assistant pastor in a small church. Humanly speaking we had very little, but the baby made us instantly rich. When her brother arrived three years later our wealth was multiplied. The psalmist certainly knew what he was talking about when, under Holy Spirit inspiration, he wrote, 'Sons are a heritage from the Lord, children a reward from him' (Psalm 127:3).

Although the apostle Paul was unmarried and unblessed by biological fatherhood, he knew how it felt to be a father. In the passage under consideration he declares that he is the Corinthians' spiritual father. He had a father's concern for their spiritual welfare. We see the Greek word *pater* reflected in such English terms as '*pater*nity' (becoming a father), '*pater*nalism' (fatherly care exercised by government over the governed) and '*pater*noster' ('our father', as in the Lord's prayer).

In 1 Corinthians 4:15 Paul introduces a contrasting term. The Corinthians only have one spiritual 'father', but there may be 'ten thousand guardians'. The word translated 'guardian' is *paidagogos* (as seen in our word 'pedagogue', a teacher who practises 'pedagogy').

Now, the difference drawn in 1 Corinthians 4:15 is based

upon relationship. Fathers have a biological responsibility. This commits them to loving concern for their children, a love which knows no holidays. There never is a time when a father is not a father. Paul explains his spiritual relationship to the Corinthians by referring to fatherhood.

On the other hand a guardian in Bible times was a slave who raised the child on behalf of the true parents. He was a sort of 'male nanny' who took the child to lessons and generally looked after its welfare. Paul intends no disparagement by his comparison in our text. The guardian exercised an important function as far as it went, but it never went as far as fatherhood.

In 1 Corinthians there are three further references to fatherhood. According to 1 Corinthians 1:3 Christians shared in the fatherhood of God. Paul never presented the fatherhood of God as a universal fact. One can only be admitted to God's family by repentance and faith. The fatherhood of God presupposes the regenerating work of his Holy Spirit and the sacrifice of his Son.

The Puritans often wrote concerning this truth. Thomas Watson said, 'The little word Father, pronounced in faith, has overcome God.' Stephen Charnock (1628-1680), the great Presbyterian divine and author of *Existence and Attributes of God*, explained it in these terms: 'The word Father is personal, the word God is essential.'

By way of total contrast, Paul paints a picture of paternal failure in 1 Corinthians 5:1. Into the church at Corinth has come gross immorality, for a man has committed adultery with his 'father's wife'. Apparently the father had remarried, perhaps as a widower. The son of a first marriage had then slept with his father's wife. In these days of total moral collapse, we can thank God that the Bible is explicit, and deals with issues which we face.

The final reference to fatherhood in 1 Corinthians speaks of the heroes of the faith, the Jewish 'forefathers were all under the cloud . . . they all passed through the sea' (1 Cor. 10:1). Those valiant Old Testament saints followed God's leading through the desert and through the Red Sea. Despite their many failings and ultimate inability to enter the promised land, Paul revered them as the 'forefathers'.

Jewish respect for ancestors was based upon their faithfulness to Jehovah. Forefathers were only great because their God was great. It is a significant contribution to Paul's view of fatherhood to link it with spiritual patriarchs. True fathers are spiritual fathers, and false fathers are those who fail to set a godly example.

Chip off the old block

In English we say a son is a 'chip off the old block', which is a tender sentiment but hardly a flattering comparison. The Germans dress the idea in a different metaphor, by saying that 'The apple does not fall far from the tree.' Both make the point that children bear more than a physical resemblance to their parents.

There are four distinct applications of the word *pater* ('father') in the New Testament. The first refers to *biological fatherhood*. The love of a father is seen in the story of Jairus, a ruler in the synagogue. He journeyed especially to ask Jesus for healing, but the Lord was delayed. Still the father believed, and the Lord raised his little daughter from the dead (Mark 5:21-43).

Another father came to Christ, and the story is found in John 4. This man was a royal functionary at Capernaum, and the Lord healed his son from a considerable distance. This led both the father and his family to believe in Messiah (John 4:43-53).

The value of godly fathers was epitomized in the writings of John Flavel, the Puritan Nonconformist, (died 1691). 'What a mercy was it to us,' Flavel wrote, 'to have parents that prayed for us before they had us, as well as in our infancy when we could not pray for ourselves!'

A second application of the word 'father' refers to *ancestors*. This idea was focused in John 8, where Jesus debated with the Pharisees. The legalists claimed Abraham as their father (John 8:39, 53). Christ even called Abraham 'your father' (John 8:56), although he made it clear that their real ancestor was that devious old devil, Satan (John 8:44).

This remarkable definition of ancestry is seen in a quote by John Garland Pollard: 'Genealogy: Tracing yourself back to people better than you are.' According to Dean Inge (1860-1954) of St Paul's Cathedral, 'A nation is a society united by a delusion about its ancestry and by common hatred of its neighbours.'

The third meaning of the word 'father' is that of *spiritual fathers*. The apostle Peter wrote of 'our fathers' who have died (2 Peter 3:4), harking back to the Jewish leaders who were godly.

Paul held up Abraham as the father of the faithful. In Romans 4:12 he focuses on the faith which Abraham exhibited even before his covenant with God was sealed by circumcision. In fact, the spiritual fatherhood of Abraham is one of the main emphases in Romans.

In his commentary on 1 Corinthians 4:15 John Calvin devotes a good deal of attention to spiritual fatherhood. Part of his comment makes this profound assertion: 'It is He [God] alone who, by His own influence, begets souls, and regenerates and quickens them. He makes use of the ministry of His servants for this purpose, and there is no harm in their being called *fathers*, in respect of this ministry.'[1]

Of course the final application of fatherhood must belong to *God* alone. In James 1:17 he is called 'the Father of heavenly lights' referring to creation. He is the 'Father of our spirits' according to Hebrews 12:9. Throughout the Gospels, Jesus claims an exclusive relationship to his Father (Matt. 11:27; John 10:30, etc.)

One of the greatest statements of God's fatherhood comes at the opening of the pattern prayer, which Jesus taught his disciples. They were instructed to pray,

> Our Father in heaven,
> hallowed be your name
> (Matt. 6:9).

1. John Calvin, *Commentary on the First Epistle to the Corinthians*, Baker Book House Edition, XX, p.172.

10.
Sex sin

'*There is* **sexual immorality** *among you*' (1 Cor. 5:1)
'*Not to associate with* **sexually immoral** *people*' (1 Cor. 5:9)
'*The people of this world who are* **immoral**' (1 Cor. 5:10)
'*Calls himself a brother but is* **sexually immoral**' (1 Cor. 5:11)

Sex is big business. In fact, pornographic literature, films and video cassettes are major items of export and import. These wicked wares are flogged openly in the streets of such cities as Copenhagen and Amsterdam. Frankfurt airport even has a sex shop indicated with a rude sign.

In recent times two major acts have passed through Parliament to control the skin trade. The abuse of children by porn publishers was attacked in the 1978 Protection of Children Bill. (Previously, children as young as seven had been put before the camera to make blue films.) A further step in the control of pornography was Tim Sainsbury's (1981) Indecent Displays (Control) Act, which has at least liberated us from the shop-window display of disgusting literature and toys.

A helpful contribution to this movement for reform came from James Anderton, Chief Constable of Greater Manchester. In conjunction with Mary Whitehouse, Anderton launched a campaign against porn. 'Pornography is a dangerous threat to family life,' the crusading Chief Constable asserted.

It is the little word 'porn' which gives us a key to the Greek text of 1 Corinthians 5. In verse 1 we have the word 'immorality' which is the Greek word *porneia*. The same root word occurs in verses 9, 10 and 11 as *pornos* ('a sexually immoral person').

In 1 Corinthians 5 the focus of biblical rebuke falls on immorality in the church. A man has taken his father's wife (that is, his step-mother) as a concubine. This act of incest violates not only the Old Testament, but also pagan sensi-

tivities. That it offended the Corinthian public shows just
how outrageous was this sin, for the Corinthians were
proverbial for their immorality.

Paul dwells heavily upon sexual sin in 1 Corinthians. For
instance, in 1 Corinthians 6:7-18 Paul warns repeatedly that
no immoral person will reach heaven. This immorality is
broadened to include homosexuality. (In our day this blanket
rejection of homosexuality is sorely needed.) In the verses of
1 Corinthians 6 Paul tackles various sexual sins: adultery and
male prostitution (v.9), prostitution (vv.15-16) and even a
sidewise reference to venereal disease (v.18).

The greatest bulwark against immorality, according to Paul,
is marriage (1 Cor. 7:2). Despite his well-known commitment
to celibacy, Paul regarded marriage as the main preventative
against immoral relations. By implication he condemned all
sexual relations outside marriage.

Immorality is also seen to be an infectious dry-rot within
society. Because of moral laxity, more than 23,000 of the
children of Israel died on one day (1 Cor. 10:8, compared
with Num. 25:1-9).

This theme carries over into 2 Corinthians where Paul still
urges Christians to abstain from sexual sin (2 Cor. 12:21). In
the early church, especially in Greece, immorality was a persistent problem, and Paul spoke out fearlessly against it.

Today within a few yards of our church there are pimps,
massage parlours, prostitutes and pornography. If we are to
be truly biblical Christians, we too must speak out against
such sin. Already this has produced threats and derision, but
God's Word is not rendered invalid by the sneers of sexual
slave-traders.

The pornographic society

Just now we are seeing a most remarkable coincidence of
events in our city. The number of sex shops has grown, and
so has the number of sexual attacks. In fact, one young lady
was attacked within a few feet of our church.

At the same time educators are advocating sex education

and experiments for children as young as five and six. A famous bishop has burst into print urging that the age of consent for sexual intercourse should be lowered to fourteen. This misguided liberal spirit only encourages the current trend towards anarchy on the moral level.

Our word *porneia* has two primary uses in the Bible. First, it is applied *literally to sexual sin*. In Ephesians 5:3 the apostle Paul warns the Ephesians, 'Among you there must not be even a hint of sexual immorality.' This commitment to purity is not natural; it must be taught. In an excellent article which appeared in the *Washington Star* (3 July 1977), Eunice Shriver, sister of President Kennedy, said, 'Intellectual virtues can be taught . . . moral virtues are formed by acts.' Christian ethics concerning sex must be trained into the young of every generation. He who hesitates to teach this truth will lose the battle in very short order.

The Lord applied our word to adultery, the practice of sex by married people outside the marriage relationship. In Mark 10:19 Jesus repeats the Ten Commandments and thus approves and enforces them. In Matthew 19:9 he shows adultery to be a cause of marital breakdown.

The danger of extra-marital sexual relations is seen daily in the media, as actors and actresses dramatize the delights of adultery without showing the disasters it causes. The dangers were stated most clearly by Professor Ian Donald of Glasgow University. 'Girls should be taught to value themselves more and not to enslave themselves to the "lusts and deceptions of male chauvinist pigs",' proclaimed the professor of midwifery. After all, he has the task of cleaning up the legacy of sorrow left by lecherous adulterers.

There is also a second use of our word, and this is the *figurative application to spiritual unfaithfulness*. In the Greek version of the Old Testament (the Septuagint), Hosea 6:10 contains this reference: 'Ephraim is given to prostitution and Israel is defiled.'

The same application is employed in Revelation. The Lord gave to the church at Thyatira 'time to repent of her immorality' (Rev. 2:21). This may apply to actual sexual sin, but in Revelation 19:2 the reference seems to be spiritually, to the 'great prostitute who corrupted the earth by her adulteries'.

This spiritual unfaithfulness emerged soon after the end of the apostolic age. One sees the fruit of it in the demise during the seventh century of the once-thriving Christian church at Thyatira. Internal rot had prepared the way for a Muslim rout of the church.

Now the major churches of Europe and North America are likewise involved in spiritual adultery. Unbiblical theology cuts away the foundation of truth and leaves the church crumbling. Unspiritual churches attract people to a show of pop music and pop preaching. Little cute sermonettes have produced a generation of Christianettes, miniatures of the real thing. Unfaithful leaders sell their souls and their pastoral charges for every conceivable reason, from political favour to imagined church unity. Lack of love for God leads to spiritual sterility.

Paul's warning is doubly necessary: 'do not associate' with sexually immoral people.

11.
God is King

'The wicked will not inherit the **kingdom** *of God'* (1 Cor. 6:9)

'The main question for any ordination candidate', Donald Grey Barnhouse (1895-1960) used to insist, 'is the proper interpretation of kingdom truth.' This begs the question of who sets the standard of proper interpretation. In Barnhouse's case it was his own rather unique view of the end times.

From the apostolic age onward, the kingdom of God has challenged the best brains among Christians. Jesus taught the coming kingdom. The apostles all assumed the kingdom would come. In successive ages church leaders have longed to penetrate its secrets. Meanwhile the best theological minds have fought over it. It is not my purpose here to propose a final solution, but rather to explore Paul's teaching concerning the kingdom as it is expressed in 1 Corinthians.

In the passage under consideration, the Greek word for 'kingdom' is *basileia*, a term which occurs 161 times in the New Testament. We also see it mirrored in several English words. The Christian name 'Basil' means literally 'king'. In Roman times a *'basil*ica' was an assembly hall, which is now applied to churches. In the upper arm is a major vein called the *'basil*ic vein' because of its prominence.

Paul's purpose in 1 Corinthians is the exposition of ethics for a city devoid of natural morality. To undergird this primary premise, Paul teaches in 1 Corinthians 6:9-10 that immoral people will not inherit God's kingdom. The list is rather explicit, and it especially condemns certain common customs of the eighties. Mentioned among the excluded are immoral people, adulterers, homosexuals, drunkards and swindlers. This reads like our daily newspaper.

Already in 1 Corinthians 4:20 Paul has taught that the kingdom of God requires righteousness. 'The kingdom of God is not a matter of talk but of power,' according to the apostle. Religious life which only produces platitudes is not biblical Christianity. There must also be the power of a changed life as an evidence of Christ's kingship. Evangelical churches stand in danger of becoming religious 'talk shops', where we dispense theologically correct sermons, but no righteous behaviour backs up all this cassette-packaged preaching.

In his great resurrection chapter, Paul again returns to the theme of the kingdom. Christ will in the end hand over 'the kingdom to God the Father after he has destroyed all dominion, authority and power' (1 Cor. 15:24). Here is trinitarian truth which reveals the ultimate glory of God the Father. In that day Christians will reign with the Son in the Father's kingdom and angels and men will be subject (1 Cor. 6:3).

The citizenship requirements for the kingdom are set out in the resurrection chapter. According to 1 Corinthians 15:50, 'Flesh and blood cannot inherit the kingdom of God, nor does the perishable inherit the imperishable.' Only those who have been transformed by the returning Christ will be fit for the kingdom. People who have remained outside his redemption will not qualify for the kingdom. It is worthy of note that Jesus taught his disciples alone to pray, 'Thy kingdom come.' For the uncommitted, the kingdom's coming is an unmitigated disaster.

The King is coming

At the beginning I said the kingdom has been a battlefield. Albert Schweitzer (1875-1975) was a prodigious organist, sacrificial doctor and dedicated missionary, but theologically he was a rank liberal. He claimed the kingdom of God had no expression in the present and only related to the coming of Christ. Meanwhile C.H. Dodd (1884-1973), the famous Oxford and Manchester New Testament scholar, surmised that the kingdom was locked up within history and had no application at all to the end times. Other theological schools, including the traditionally evangelical views of premillennialism,

amillennialism and postmillennialism, range somewhere
between Schweitzer and Dodd.

Our purpose in this little volume is to consider the meaning
of the kingdom for us. First of all the kingdom is related to
God. We find the *'kingdom of God'* seventy-one times in the
New Testament. At the end of the Sermon on the Mount,
Jesus taught his disciples to 'seek first his kingdom and his
righteousness, and all these things will be given to you as well'
(Matt. 6:33). The spiritual nature of the kingdom is taught in
Romans 14:17: 'For the kingdom of God is not a matter of
eating and drinking, but of righteousness, peace and joy in
the Holy Spirit.' We may thus conclude that the kingdom of
God is a spiritual reality and not to be confused with a now
visible realm.

George E. Ladd, the late Professor of Theology at Fuller
Theological Seminary, wrote this concerning the kingdom:
'While the kingdom of God as the realm in which God's will
is perfectly done continues to be future, the Kingdom as the
active saving power of God has come into the world in the
person and activity of Christ to redeem men from the kingdom
of Satan.'

A second connection of our word is the *kingdom of heaven*.
Both John the Baptist and Jesus preached the simple message:
'Repent, for the kingdom of heaven is near' (Matt. 3:2; 4:17).
Many seem to equate the kingdom of heaven with the kingdom of God, but a study of the texts would indicate that this
is the perfected kingdom. No pride (Matt. 18:1-4), lawlessness
(Matt. 5:19), hypocrisy (Matt. 7:21), or any sin shall be
tolerated in the kingdom of heaven. Its mysteries are still
hidden from human eyes (Matt. 13:11). Evidently the kingdom of heaven is the perfected state of God's rule, whereas
the kingdom of God and the church are still imperfect.

Another aspect of the kingdom is the *kingdom of David*.
In Mark 11:10 this kingdom is described as a glorious future
event ushered in by the Lord's coming. In this revived kingdom of David the Lord will rule unhindered.

In the later apostolic age the writers used the *'kingdom of
the Lord'*. Peter devoted much of his second letter to the
'eternal kingdom of our Lord and Saviour Jesus Christ' (2 Peter

1:11). An echo of this idea is found in the final letter of Paul, where he rejoices in this comfort: 'The Lord will rescue me from every evil attack and will bring me safely to his heavenly kingdom. To him be glory for ever and ever' (2 Tim. 4:18).

As Professor Ladd wrote, 'The diversity of New Testament data has led to diverse interpretations' concerning the kingdom.[1] Although I have no desire to oversimplify profound theological questions, there are some truths which are held by most serious students of Scripture.

First, the kingdom is a dynamic fact. God is already building his kingdom and it grows daily. Second, the kingdom will include a final defeat of Satan and his banishment from the arena of human affairs. Third, the coming of Christ created this kingdom through his redemptive work. Fourth, the kingdom is the logical and eternal conclusion of God's sovereignty.

The disciples' final question to Jesus was related to the kingdom: 'Lord, are you at this time going to restore the kingdom to Israel?' (Acts 1:6.) The Lord's answer was a qualified 'No'. The kingdom of God is much bigger than Israel. It embraces a multitude of Gentiles, too, who recognize Jesus as King of kings and Lord of lords.

1. *Zondervan Pictorial Bible Dictionary*, p.466.

12.
Body language

'The **body** *is not meant for sexual immorality but for the Lord, and the Lord for the* **body***'* (1 Cor. 6:13)
'Your **body** *is a temple of the Holy Spirit'* (1 Cor. 6:19)
'Honour God with your **body***'* (1 Cor. 6:20)

The body is real, and there is no doubt about that. After a surprise snowstorm we dash out to clear away the snow. Since we in England seldom shovel snow, this sudden exercise is an experience in awareness. We become aware of muscles long forgotten, or that we never knew we had. Moving is such a painful experience that our bodies become the centre of attention.

In 1 Corinthians Paul teaches some basic truth regarding the body. The Greek word which occurs repeatedly in this context is *soma* (body). It is also reflected in such English terms as 'psycho*somatic*', an illness which affects the body but is caused by the mind. Less familiar is the adjective '*soma*tic', and a 'somatic cell' is the basic building block of the body. The study of this basic body construction is called '*soma*tology'. *Soma* refers to the body as a whole.

In 1 Corinthians 6 there are several references to the body. The Christian's body belongs to the Lord. This is stated in 1 Corinthians 6:13 as axiomatic: 'The body is not meant for sexual immorality, but for the Lord, and the Lord for the body.' Much ancient philosophy regarded the body as being less valuable than the spirit. The ultimate aim for Plato and his intellectual disciples was the liberation of the spirit from the body. Death became a friend because the spirit would escape from its physical prison.

Paul extended his teaching to include ethics. Because the Christian's body belongs to God, the Christian should not unite his body sexually to that of a prostitute (1 Cor. 6:16). Sexual intercourse creates a physical bond, as the creation story states (Gen. 2:24). Therefore the Christian must never enter into forbidden sexual relationships, but only that union sanctified by the God-ordained marriage bond.

Sexual sin violates the body of the one who commits it. 'All other sins a man commits are outside his body,' Paul postulates, 'but he who sins sexually sins against his body' (1 Cor. 6:18). Augustine, as a young man, engaged in sexual sin and fathered an illegitimate child. After his conversion one of his former lovers spotted him on the street. 'Augustine, it is I, it is I!' she called out as she pursued him down the street. Finally Augustine turned and said, 'Yes, but it is not I.' The Lord had liberated him and forgiven him.

Advancing from the ethical aspect, Paul introduces a magnificent theme to clinch his spiritual instruction: 'Your body is a temple of the Holy Spirit' (1 Cor. 6:19). For this reason Christians are to 'honour God with your body' (1 Cor. 6:20). Christians possess their bodies as a gift from God, and they give them back to him for his purposes.

As Paul often does in his epistles, he summarizes this teaching with an unforgettable statement: 'We would prefer to be away from the body and at home with the Lord' (2 Cor. 5:8). When our body has been buried we shall give account to the Lord, and our account will cover the activities carried out while we were in the body. To put it in Pauline terms: 'We must all appear before the judgement seat of Christ, that each one may receive what is due to him for the things done while in the body, whether good or bad' (2 Cor. 5:10).

But burial, or burning, is not the end of the body. Paul predicates his whole teaching on the significance of the body by reference to resurrection. 'The body is sown a natural body, it is raised a spiritual body' (1 Cor. 15:44). The body is eternally important to God (Rom. 8:23); its redemption will crown our adoption as his children.

Body building

When I was a boy the comic magazines abounded with advertisements for 'body-building' programmes. Charles Atlas was the star of these. He had taken the course and been transformed from a weakling to a veritable powerhouse. My problem was not being a weakling. I was a 'husky' lad, or fat, if you press me for honesty! All hopes of my being an Atlas seemed beyond the scope of any body-building scheme.

The Bible puts a whole new interpretation on body building. Our word *soma* speaks first of the *human body*. In his Sermon on the Mount Jesus warned us not to supplant spiritual priorities with physical pursuits: 'Therefore I tell you, do not worry about your life, what you will eat or drink; or about your body, what you will wear. Is not life more important than food, and the body more important than clothes?' (Matt. 6:25.)

Despite this warning against preoccupation with things, the incarnation of Jesus gave incredible dignity to the human body. His earthly body was elevated to a higher position than the temple at Jerusalem (John 2:21).

It is the human body which is most often described by our Greek word. However, the body is placed on a much higher plane by Christ than it was by other ancient religions. Even after death the Christian honours the body by properly caring for it and burying it. Joseph of Arimathea and Nicodemus took the body of Jesus and embalmed it before burying it (John 19:38-42). Now the tomb and crucifixion site are in the hands of a British evangelical trust. Although Catholic tradition disputes the location, true Christians often feel that Gordon's Calvary might well be the place of Christ's crucifixion and the nearby tomb the scene of his brief burial.

A second use of our word is unusual. In Colossians 2:17 the word *soma* is translated *'reality'*. In Paul's words, traditional religious practices and feasts are 'a shadow of things that were to come; the reality' (body), 'however, is found in Christ'. The idea is the familiar contrast between dreaming and being awake. A dream, be it good or bad, seems so real. The physical symptoms of fear emerge and we feel them acutely. Then we awaken. The perspiration still stands out on our brow, and the bedding is disturbed by our girations. But the event which we dreamed about is only a fantasy. The reality is our body and the bed. All of the religious practices which preceded Christ were like a dream in comparison with the reality of his presence.

There is, of course, a third use of our word *soma*. It is the *church* of Jesus Christ. In Colossians 1:18 Christ is described as the 'head of the body, the church'. Also in Ephesians 4:4 church unity is summarized by reference to 'one body and one Spirit'. Of course, the Corinthian letter also draws this comparison between the human body and the church (1 Cor. 12:12-13). All believers are baptized into this spiritual body. It is Christ's body on earth, the hands and feet that do his work (Rom. 12:4).

The church of Jesus Christ is not simply an organization. It is not synonymous or co-extensive with a vast machine like the Roman Catholic Church, boasting millions of members. Neither is it identical with the cosy little house fellowships which have sprung up in our time. No, the body of Christ is not an organization, but rather an organism. It is capable of immense variety and vitality, it has been seen among the apostolic ancients and our computerized contemporaries. It is present in the formal worship of European church traditions and in the cultural clothing of missionary stations. The body of Christ cannot be contained by our traditions, or anyone else's. Praise God for that!

13.
Married bliss

*'Better to **marry** than to burn with passion'* (1 Cor. 7:9)

Marriage is a matter of perpetual interest. Obviously human history moves forward on the wheels of marriage. The Bible contains numerous references to marriage, from Adam and Eve onwards.

The actual marriage ceremony was a product of Jewish custom and culture. As reflected in the Old and New Testaments, the wedding was based upon a contractual agreement entered into at betrothal. On the appointed day the bridegroom went to the house of the bride and brought her home to his dwelling. Festivities filled several days.

As Christian customs developed there emerged a wedding ceremony, possibly by the fourth or fifth century. By the end of the first Christian millennium Pope Gregory (1023-85) was declaring marriage to be sacramental, and this viewpoint prevailed at the Council of Trent (1562).

The Reformers regarded marriage as a biblical state, but not a sacrament. Martin Luther asserted that marriage was devoid of sacramental meaning, and John Calvin stated it even more clearly: 'While we all admit it [marriage] to be an institution of God, no man ever saw [it] to be a sacrament, until the time of Gregory.'[1]

The Greek verb which means 'to marry' is *gameo*. It occurs in the verb form only twenty-six times in the New Testament, and there are a further sixteen occurrences of the noun *gamos*, 'marriage' or 'wedding'. We see the root of this word in such English terms as 'mono*gamy*' (marriage to one person) or 'poly*gamy*' (marriage to more than one person). There are, of course, more obscure words such as '*gamo*genesis', meaning 'sexual reproduction'.

Our Greek word occurs in 1 Corinthians 7. In conceding the necessity for marriage, Paul writes, 'But if they cannot control themselves, they should marry, for it is better to marry than to burn with passion' (1 Cor. 7:9). When we view the machinations of many young people today and the sexual perversion which often accompanies promiscuity, we see the wisdom of this apostolic assertion. Marriage certainly channels sexual energy into more profitable paths. Any pastor who is called upon to mop up the mess caused by sex without sanctity can whole-heartedly concur with Paul's proposition.

When discussing the role of single people in the church, Paul returns to this theme. 'If you do marry, you have not sinned,' Paul teaches, 'but those who marry will face many troubles in this life' (1 Cor. 7:28, 33). Although marriage is the answer to being overwhelmed with sexual desire, marriage does not solve all problems. It restricts freedom for both partners, it places financial responsibilities on people, it unites people for life (divorce notwithstanding), to name only a few consequences.

The apostle Paul adjudged that he had a greater degree of freedom to serve God because of his singleness (1 Cor. 7:7, 29-34). This statement together with others led some church fathers, such as Tertullian and Jerome, to advocate celibacy. This practice was enshrined in monasticism and lives on in the celibacy of Roman Catholic priests and nuns. Although Paul argued powerfully for the single life of service, he firmly condemned any prohibition of marriage (1 Tim. 4:3) as a doctrine taught by demons.

The third general statement concerning our word *gameo* (to marry) is the propriety of marriage. Evidently some saints became engaged but never married, thus causing distress. To them Paul wrote, 'If anyone thinks he is acting improperly towards the virgin he is engaged to, and if she is getting along in years and he feels he ought to marry, he should do as he wants' (1 Cor. 7:36). Although the reference to 'getting along in years' is scriptural, it may not be the tactful thing to use in conversation with a woman, or a man. Paul here gives a corrective method for the loose courtship practices of our day.

In our day we see young people moving with blinding speed from one girl-friend to another, or one young man to another. The result is heartache and disappointment. Marriage is often not intended, nor would it be appropriate in many such cases. Surely Paul would here condemn such loose customs, be they the casual flirtation or the sexual experiment.

Marriage in Paul's writings is a sacred privilege. He uses it as a picture of Christ's union with the church. Against the black backdrop of pagan Corinth, Paul paints the picture of serious and saintly marriage.

Happy though married

In our day the questions of marriage, divorce and remarriage are much discussed. No Christian minister or church can avoid dealing with them. Each year adultery, brutality and incompatibility catapult thousands out of marriage and into the doldrums of divorce.

Church leaders are seriously polarized in their viewpoints concerning divorce. In expounding the Sermon on the Mount, Dr Lloyd-Jones followed Calvin's exposition in concluding that in cases of adultery 'divorce has ended the marriage . . . and this innocent man is entitled to re-marriage'.[2] Meanwhile, many churches and ministers do not feel free to remarry divorced people or admit them to office in the church.

No matter what position one takes on the above issue, the Bible presents marriage as a serious, lifelong union. The verb *gameo* (to marry) is wed to three subjects in Bauer's *Greek-English Lexicon*. First, the *man marries*. In the above-mentioned passage of the Sermon on the Mount, the man is seen as the initiator of marriage (Matt. 5:32; Luke 16:18). The impression given is that of a unilateral decision by the man, but Scripture will correct this as we proceed.

The Puritan preacher and penman Henry Smith (1560-91) achieved great spiritual excellence in his thirty-one years. Some of his statements on marriage are priceless. 'To direct thee to a right choice,' Smith said, 'the Holy Ghost gives thee two rules in the choice of a wife, godliness and fitness.' In a similar vein he wrote: 'First, he must choose his love, and then he must love his choice.'

However, the *woman* is also a subject of the verb 'to marry'.

In Mark 10:12 it is the woman who divorces and remarries. When writing about widows, Paul urges young widows to marry and raise a family. Thus they are not a financial burden to the church (1 Tim. 5:11, 14).

From a purely linguistic standpoint, as well as a practical one, the woman is not viewed as being passive in the marriage act. One recalls the statement of the Prince of Wales when he proposed in February 1981 to the now Princess of Wales. 'She has agreed to have me,' the Prince said with a degree of astonishment. Then the world was treated to that magnificent wedding ceremony in which Charles and Diana promised to live together in loving marriage.

The third application of our word is more passive, *to be married*. (It is almost like a related verb, *gamizo*, 'to give in marriage'.) After his great pronouncement on marriage, the Lord was greeted by the implied question: 'If this is the situation between a husband and wife, it is better not to marry' (Matt. 19:10). When the Lord discussed the afterlife, he taught that there would be no 'marrying or giving in marriage' (Matt. 22:30). Angels were not wed, and neither shall we be in the life to come. One final reference underlines this general application. In the end times there will be un-bridled 'marrying and giving in marriage' as there was in Noah's time (Matt. 24:38).

In our day divorce and remarriage are gaining momentum. Dr Jack Dominian, senior psychiatrist at London's Central Middlesex Hospital, estimated in 1980 that one marriage in five will end in the divorce courts. He also computed that divorce costs the country about £1,000 million annually in legal, medical and social service costs. Surely we who claim Christ as Lord must devote our energies to preaching, counselling and encouraging biblical standards of married life.

1. John Calvin, *Institutes of the Christian Religion*, book IV, chapter 19.
2. D.M. Lloyd-Jones, *Sermon on the Mount*, IVP, p.265.

14.
Virgin virtue

'Now about **virgins***'* (1 Cor. 7:25)
'If a **virgin** *marries, she has not sinned'* (1 Cor. 7:28)
*'***Virgin** *is concerned about the Lord's affairs'* (1 Cor. 7:34)

Single life has become a boom topic in our age. Many simply ignore the subject and thrust their heads into the sand like ostriches. 'It's a feminist issue,' some say, 'women are trying to break out of the bonds of marriage into the supposed single liberty.'

Others see the single life as a temporary phenomenon. They reason that most 'normal' people really want to be married, and given time they will 'marry and settle down'. Single people are regarded as being immature, impractical and unstable.

A vicious streak also colours the viewpoint of some concerning single adults. One single missionary told me he had repeatedly been accused of homosexuality by other Christians. This was a particularly destructive label and libel against that young man.

By contrast with such modern misapprehensions, the New Testament presents a well-defined doctrine of single life. The apostle Paul in 1 Corinthians considers singleness under the term 'virgins'. (Other Scriptures reveal that this term embraces both women and men, compare Rev. 14:4.) The Greek word for 'virgin' is *parthenos*. It is seen in the name of the Parthenon temple built by Athenians in 447-432 B.C. and dedicated to their patron goddess Athena. In 426 A.D. the Parthenon became a Christian temple dedicated to Saint Sophia, and in 662 it became a shrine to the Virgin Mary. (Thus the name Parthenon took on temporary, and indeed tenuously, Christian connotations).

In the New Testament, however, the term 'virgin' is remarkably free from religious overtones. It simply designates an unmarried and chaste person, usually a woman. In 1 Corinthians 7:25 the apostle Paul introduces instructions concerning virgins. He remarks that these instructions are neither Jewish in origin nor are they a 'command from the Lord', that is a direct teaching of Christ. This does not rob them of apostolic authority and divine inspiration, however. In fact, Paul includes a formula designed to denote inspiration: 'as one who by the Lord's mercy is trustworthy' (compare with 1 Tim. 1:15; Titus 3:8). Paul knew he was writing revelation.

In defending the single life, Paul added that 'If a virgin marries, she has not sinned. But those who marry will face many troubles' (1 Cor. 7:28). To put it conversely: those who remain single are spared from many troubles. To focus this teaching, one can think of the life insurance which a married man carries to care for his wife and children in case of his early demise. This principle of care can be extended to many other spheres of life. A single person does not bear these responsibilities.

Paul does not dwell on the material and personal cares from which a single person is delivered, but rather the apostle states spiritual reasons for singleness. The single person 'is concerned about the Lord's affairs' (1 Cor. 7:34). This is obviously an idealization, because not all single Christians are spiritually minded, nor all married Christians worldly. Paul here simply presents the *advantage* which single Christians should have in this respect.

One recalls another single missionary colleague in Germany. She devoted her life and considerable learning so selflessly that many young people were indelibly marked by her devoted attitude to Christian work. The honour roll of single, spiritual nobility includes such women as Amy Carmichael (1867-1951), Frances Ridley Havergal (1838-79) and Gladys Aylward (1900-70).

Also in this passage the apostle Paul pursues the question of fathers giving their (virgin) daughters in marriage. Although he prefers to see the virgin daughter remain single, Paul concedes, 'He who gives his virgin in marriage does right' (1 Cor. 7:36-38, NIV marginal reading). Of course, the first-century customs dictated arranged marriages, but Paul makes the point here that singleness is preferred, although not prescribed for Christians.

There seems to be a connection between the crisis in Corinth (1 Cor. 7:26) and the apostolic advice in favour of celibacy. Elsewhere Paul strongly opposes any prohibition of marriage (1 Tim. 4:3) as a demonic teaching. While Paul preferred singleness, he never prohibited marriage but rather recognized that 'each man has his own gift from God; one has this gift, another has that' (1 Cor. 7:7).

Single blessedness

In teaching young people the absolute necessity of marrying a Christian, one preacher proclaimed, 'It's better to remain single than to marry a non-believer.' Then he put a pretty fine point on it: 'It's better to endure single blessedness than double cussedness.'

In our society singleness is often looked down upon, and when beauty begins to fade many single people become victims of the 'last train syndrome'. As friends find their way to the altar a mild depression sets in. Finally it turns to blind panic. The first likely lad or lassie to come along is accepted, and the hasty marriage soon turns to leisurely repentance.

But the biblical picture of singleness is much more positive than this parody of present practice. There are three distinct applications of the word 'virgin' in the Bible. The first is obviously the application to *single adults*. Jesus told the parable of the wise and foolish virgins in Matthew 25:1-13. These were wedding guests involved in giving their friend a send-off into wedded bliss. Any pastor knows these young adults who attend the marriage of friends and personally convey their best wishes.

In Luke 2:36 there is a rather difficult reference to Anna, 'who lived with her husband for seven years after her marriage' (literally 'from her virginity, *parthenias*'). What a woman she was! Having been a chaste virgin, she became a faithful wife and a prophetic widow.

The apostle Paul refers to the four daughters of the evangelist Philip. His daughters were virgin prophetesses (Acts 21:9). One cannot but see the spiritual atmosphere which permeated that home in Caesarea. The dedication of a father is seen in the ministry of his daughters. Even today many men who spend themselves in the Lord's service see the reward of godly children.

Our word 'virgin' is even applied to chaste young men in Revelation 14:4. Although these appear to be spiritually special people, and the location of their service is heaven, one still feels that they are real men who have remained chaste.

A second use of the word 'virgin' is specific and *messianic*. In the Septuagint Greek Old Testament the prophetic promise of a 'virgin-born' Messiah is given through Isaiah (Isa. 7:14). This word is repeated in Matthew 1:23 when Mary is identified as 'the virgin'.

The virgin birth of Christ was identified in the early part of our century as one of the fundamentals of biblical Christianity. (These fundamentals were presented in a series of booklets which appeared in the years 1910-15 in the United States. Three million copies were sent free, one to every theological student and Christian worker who could be found. This is how our modern word 'Fundamentalism' came into being.)

Even a theologically questionable writer like Karl Barth saw that the church is not at liberty 'to convert the doctrine of the Virgin Birth into an option for specially strong or for specially weak souls'.[1]

A third application of the word 'virgin' refers spiritually to the *church of Jesus Christ*. In 2 Corinthians 11:2 the apostle Paul sees his task as that of presenting Christians 'as a pure virgin' to Christ. This metaphor is applied to Israel in Isaiah 62:5, and the book of Revelation (21:2) contains another reference in eschatological terms. Paul spoke in Ephesians 5:25-27 of Christ's sanctifying work to present to himself the Christians as 'a radiant church, without stain or wrinkle or any other blemish, but holy and blameless' (Ephesians 5:27).

Dr R.T. Kendall, minister of Westminster Chapel, sees the genius of Christianity in its fitting of saints for heaven. 'Faith ultimately derives its source and motivation from this,' according to Dr Kendall, 'we are going to Heaven — and know it.'[2]

Surely the wedding portrait of a virgin church, undefiled by intercourse with the world, is a glimpse of glory. In that day the old hymn will sum up our experience:

> The Bride eyes not her garment,
> But her dear Bridegroom's face,
> I will not gaze at glory,
> But on my King of grace.
> Not at the crown He giveth,
> But on His pierced hand,
> The Lamb is all the glory
> Of Immanuel's land
>
> (Anne Ross Cousin).

1. K. Barth, *Church Dogmatics*, vol.i, part 2, p.181.
2. R.T. Kendall, *Who By Faith*, p.67.

15.
Amiable weakness

'Since their conscience is **weak**' (1 Cor. 8:7)
'A stumbling-block to the **weak**' (1 Cor. 8:9)
'**Weak** *brother, for whom Christ died'* (1 Cor. 8:11)

In the eighteenth century the novelist and magistrate Henry Fielding (1707-54) coined the phrase: 'the more amiable weakness of mankind'. To him this meant that every person deserved a chance to 'quit the directions of prudence, and follow the blind guidance of predominant passion'. In other words, sowing wild oats was a legitimate and completely excusable pursuit.

When the Bible portrays weakness, however, the emphasis falls elsewhere. Human weakness is not a euphemism for sin, but rather an occasion for the operation of divine power. So Paul's persistent pain made room for God's grace to shine out in glory. Mary Magdalene's chequered past only spotlighted the perfection of Christ. The callow youth Timothy was enabled to serve by God's call and commission.

The word used in the New Testament for 'weakness' is *astheneia*, and it also appears in the verb form *astheneo* (to be weak) and the noun *asthenes* (a weak person). Its transference to modern English is very obscure, and it appears in such medical terms as 'asthenia' (loss of strength) or an 'asthenic' (the person who is weakened). In its various forms the word appears fifty-two times in the New Testament, of which fifteen are in 1 and 2 Corinthians.

God actually succeeds in turning the tables on weakness. From a human standpoint weakness is negative, but God regards it as positive. The apostle Paul teaches that the Christian who has a weak conscience is one who has not fully developed spiritual insights (1 Cor. 8:7,10,12). Rather than looking down on such saints, stronger Christians are to protect them and actually adapt to them (1 Cor. 8:9). The reason

behind this is profound: Christ died for the weaker as well as
the more robust Christian (1 Cor. 8:11). Christianity is a corporate faith, so I bear responsibility for every other Christian.
Here is the booming biblical answer to Cain's question: 'Am I
my brother's keeper?' (Gen. 4:9.)

Tracing our word 'weakness' through the Corinthian letters,
we discover an amazing pattern. When God calls people to
serve him, he chooses weak people so that his glory will shine
through (1 Cor. 1:25-31). As Paul set about evangelizing he
became weak in appearance and action to communicate the
gospel to weak people (1 Cor. 9:22). No triumphalism tainted
the apostolic mission.

A sobering twist to this portrayal of weakness is found in
1 Corinthians 11:30. Those who come to the Lord's Table
harbouring sin against another Christian run the risk of
divine discipline. One aspect of this is physical weakness and
death.

However, when Paul wrote 2 Corinthians he returned to
the paradoxical portrayal of weakness. The apostle actually
boasted of his weakness, because it was the occasion for a
fuller revelation of Christ (2 Cor. 11:29-30). In our day of
superchurches led by pastoral superstars who (in USA, at
least) dazzle superaudiences by television, one loses the aspect
of weakness to which Paul here refers. One wonders if the
spiritual weakness of our day is not a product of the proud
image which our superleaders radiate.

Paul not only appeared weak, he was weak. The illness
which dogged his steps, and was not even removed after
prayer, left him weak. But the apostle saw this physical weakness as a vacuum into which God's strength could be poured.
So, God's power 'is made perfect in weakness'. Paul 'boasts'
about weakness and 'delights' in weakness (2 Cor. 12:9-10).
'For when I am weak,' he concludes, 'then I am strong'
(2 Cor. 12:10). Who of us would willingly submit to weakness
in order that Christ's strength might be displayed? Instead we
adopt a stance of strength, and spiritual weakness results.

Even the Lord Jesus in his humiliation shared human weakness. When he was humbled by crucifixion he shared human
weakness. Now God's power is revealed in his resurrection

glory (2 Cor. 13:4).

In his inimitable style and succinctness Thomas à Kempis (c.1380-1471), the great German mystic writer, stated scriptural truth in unforgettable terms: 'The acknowledgement of our weakness is the first step towards repairing our loss.'

Weak at the knees

The great philosopher, scientist, inventor and Christian Blaise Pascal (1623-1662) in his *Pensées* commented on most subjects, and weakness also came into the purview of his mind. 'Man is only a reed, the weakest thing in nature,' he wrote, 'but he is a thinking reed.'

Weakness in the New Testament is capable of broad interpretation. First, it refers to physical weakness, *sickness*. In fact, our word is often translated 'sick' or 'infirm'. Christ's great manifesto for social action in Matthew 25 contains this statement: 'I was sick' ('weak') 'and you looked after me' (Matt. 25:36). Here Christ urges care for the physically infirm. His disciples heeded this injunction and healed the cripple at the temple gate. In Acts 4:9 'cripple' is a translation of our word 'weak'.

It is remarkable how many men of spiritual power were marked by physical and even nervous weakness. One thinks of the great Victorian preacher Charles Haddon Spurgeon, who suffered physical pain and nervous strain and died at fifty-seven, a young age even in the nineteenth century.

Weakness is also seen in *economic* terms. Christ commended financial aid to the 'weak' (Acts 20:35). This is also the implication of Pauline teaching in 1 Thessalonians 5:14. In his provocative book, *Built as a City*, Bishop David Sheppard devoted much space to the 'powerless', those who have no economic or social pressure to exert. Surely this, too, is a focus for Christian concern in our age.

In the New Testament weakness also refers to *ethics*. Paul explored this truth in Romans. 'We who are strong ought to bear with the failings of the weak' (Rom. 15:1). The inability of men to endure moral stress is prominent in the teaching of the Lord. 'The spirit is willing, but the body is weak', he taught the disciples in Gethsemane' (Matt. 26:41).

One sees this moral weakness all around. The ex-alcoholic dares never touch drink, because the danger of addiction is always present. Gamblers who have escaped that financial rat-race dare not have the proverbial 'little flutter'. Weakness of conscience is also seen in such current problems as pornography, narcotics and the low moral tone of so many television programmes.

Another application of the word refers to the source of much of this weakness. This is *demonic weakness*. The doctor Luke referred to Mary Magdalene as a victim of 'evil spirits and diseases' (literally 'weaknesses') (Luke 8:2). Later on there is another reference to a woman who was 'crippled' (literally 'weakened') 'by a spirit for eighteen years' (Luke 13:11). We dare not discount the power of Satan in causing physical and emotional weakness. Christ surely did not.

The great truth of the Bible, however, is that weakness may be exchanged for strength. Our physical, economic, moral and satanically stimulated weakness can be swallowed up in Christ's omnipotent strength.

16.
Apostolic age

'Am I not an **apostle***?'* (1 Cor. 9:1)
*'The right to take a believing wife along with us, as do the
other* **apostles***'* (1 Cor. 9:5)

Apostles came from among Christ's companions, and they made their mark on the first century. In fact, the period from Pentecost until the death of the apostle John is called the 'apostolic age'. During that period, the message of Jesus Christ was propagated primarily through the apostles.

The Acts of the Apostles revolves initially around Peter and John, and then around Paul. James, the Lord's brother, who seems to have led the church in Jerusalem, also features prominently.

History adds accounts of the other apostles. We are indebted to John Fox (1517-1587) and his *Book of Martyrs* for collecting traditional evidence about the other apostles. Philip was crucified in Upper Asia. James the Less had his brains 'dashed out with a fuller's club' in Jerusalem. Mark was dragged through the streets of Alexandria. Thomas was speared to death in India. Simon Zelotes preached in Mauritania until his crucifixion.[1]

The Greek word we here consider is *apostolos* ('apostle'). Its connections to English are so obvious as to preclude further comment. Occuring seventy-eight times in the New Testament, the 'apostolic' title is one of the great story-shapers of the New Testament.

The word 'apostle' means literally 'sent one'. The apostles were sent out by the Lord. But they were sent out for a special purpose. In my first part-time job the departmental manager told me, 'Wayne, just keep yourself busy. Look as though you're doing something, even when there is nothing to do.' The apostles were not sent out just to 'look busy', but rather they were sent out for the business of heralding Christ's lordship.

In our passage of 1 Corinthians 9 there are several powerful statements about apostles. First, the apostle's ministry is
an *assured role*. 'Am I not an apostle?' (1 Cor. 9:1), Paul
writes, expecting the answer, 'Yes.' Although Paul knew
spiritual humility, he was also capable of a boldness borne of
divine calling.

In the next verse (1 Cor. 9:2) we see a *personal ministry*.
'I may not be an apostle to others,' Paul concedes, but 'surely
I am to you.' Paul's apostleship was confirmed in the Corin-
thians' conversion and consolidation into a church. They
were the 'seal of his apostleship' (1 Cor. 9:2). The proof of a
ministry is always people, and one thinks of the thousands of
Londoners who were touched by the ministry of Dr Lloyd-
Jones at Westminster Chapel.

There is also in this chapter a *married ministry*. Paul alludes
to the marriage of Cephas (Peter) and the Lord's brothers
(1 Cor. 9:5). This simply shatters the traditional celibacy of
Roman Catholic priesthood. If Peter is claimed as the first
Bishop of Rome, he was surely a married bishop.

Farther along in 1 Corinthians we discover that the apostles
exercised a *gifted ministry*. One of God's grace gifts to the
church was that of apostles (1 Cor. 12:28-29). With no written New Testament, the apostles were God's channel of
revelation during the years immediately following Christ's
ascension.

The apostles also exercised a convinced or *persuaded
ministry*. One of the main qualifications was an encounter
with the resurrected Lord either before or after his return to
heaven (1 Cor. 15:7-9). Paul's Damascus Road meeting with
the Lord thus qualified him for apostleship.

In 2 Corinthians Paul speaks of the danger of a *counterfeit
ministry*. Portraying themselves as 'super-apostles' (2 Cor.
11:5), these charlatans dealt in deceit (2 Cor. 11:13). Surely
in our day we find a plethora of false apostles leading everything from cults to modern house groups. Their spiritual
tyranny has plunged many sincere souls into deep distress.

A final reference to apostleship is the assertion of a *proven
ministry*. According to the apostle Paul, the marks of an
apostle are 'signs, wonders and miracles' (2 Cor. 12:12).

Quick wits of our day often say cheekily, 'Put your money where your mouth is.' Paul similarly challenged the false apostles to 'put their miracles where their mouth was'.

Apostolic succession

From Tertullian (170-220) and Cyprian (200-258) onwards certain Christians have taught 'apostolic succession'. The idea is this: there is a continuous line of descent from the original apostles to present-day priests. This connection is transmitted through consecration or ordination by bishops.

Of course, this teaching is mainly maintained by the Roman Catholic Church and the Church of England. It has come to the fore in current ecumenical considerations. Serious Anglicans and Catholics find it hard to accept a minister who has not been consecrated by an apostolic successor, no matter what theological school he represents. Many free churchmen like me see the true apostolic succession in those who declare the apostolic message as contained in the New Testament.

There are three applications of 'apostle' in the New Testament. First, it refers to first-century *agents of Christian preaching*. Strictly the circle of apostleship was drawn around the Twelve, the Lord's disciples (Matt. 10:2-4; Acts 1:26). Later on the circle was widened to include others such as Barnabas (Acts 14:14), James (Gal. 1:19), Silas and Timothy (1 Thess. 1:1, compared with 2:6-7).

When Judas committed suicide, the need arose to appoint another apostle. After discussion two names were proposed: Joseph called Barsabbas and Matthias (Acts 1:23). By prayer and casting lots, Matthias was chosen (Acts 1:24-26) to take over the apostolic ministry. However, he disappeared from the pages of Scripture along with most of the Twelve.

The work of apostles was designed to found and foster churches. They were trained by the Lord to preach the gospel message and sent out to declare his lordship (Mark 3:14). As churches were formed the apostles also took on an administrative role and formed basic policy at the Jerusalem Council (Acts 15:2). By writing the New Testament Scriptures the apostles and their close associates also gave a literary basis for future churches (Eph. 2:20). The work of the apostles in the first century cannot be overestimated, but their work seems to have ceased with the death of their longest living member, John.

A second use of the word 'apostle' is a *simple messenger*. Epaphroditus was the 'messenger' ('apostle') the Philippians sent to help Paul in prison (Phil. 2:25). The basic meaning of the word is clear. He was sent, and he had a specific assignment.

One further appearance is significant, for *the Lord Himself* is called 'the apostle and high priest whom we confess' (Heb. 3:1). In the Lord the idea of apostleship is elevated to a completely different level. He was sent by the Father (John 20:21) with the task of redeeming us. This apostleship was not capable of imitation, even by the spiritual giants of the first century.

Although the apostles are long gone, I believe one important aspect of apostleship remains. It is not seen in the elaborate trappings of the episcopate, but rather in the itinerant mandate of modern missions. These godly people are sent by the Lord with a message to proclaim. Their aim is not spiritual tyranny (like the pseudo-apostles of Christianity's lunatic fringe), but rather the sincere and powerful preaching of the gospel and the planting of indigenous churches.

1. Fox, *Book of Martyrs*, pp.2-5.

17.
Rewarding service

'If I preach voluntarily, I have a **reward***'* (1 Cor. 9:17)
'What then is my **reward***?'* (1 Cor. 9:18)

'Virtue hath her rewards', wrote Virgil (70-19 B.C.), 'and mortality her tears.'[1] Here the literary patriarch propounds a principle borne out in everyday life. A virtuous deed demands no external reward, because it is in itself a reward. This idea is biblical, even though it precedes the New Testament.

The Greek word for 'reward' is *misthos*. Its linguistic family is unusually large. A day-labourer in ancient Greece was called a *misthios* (Luke 15:17, 19, 21). He worked for cash in hand, which in those days involved no tax evasion. The price of rent was called *misthoma* (Acts 28:30). A hired hand in the fishing business was known as a *misthotos* (Mark 1:20; John 10:12).

It is the narrower use of 'reward' which attracts our attention in 1 Corinthians. In 1 Corinthians 9:17 Paul refers to the reward attached to voluntary preaching. He has built a case for support of a preacher in 1 Corinthians 9:1-15, a case not weakened by the fact that he renounced the right to income at Corinth in order to be self-supporting. Of course, the support of ministers is a source of instant opinion. Recently a Church of England vicar's wife wrote to the *Times* (3 March 1982) lamenting the 'uncaring and faceless bureaucracy' of the church. This concern over clergy incomes could be illustrated in virtually every denomination. It is no wonder that Paul emphasizes the responsibility of those taught to support their teachers in Christ.

In the same context, however, Paul argues that the privilege of preaching is his primary reward (1 Cor. 9:18). To use the Lord's phrase, 'My food is to do the will of him who sent me' (John 4:34). German evangelicals have a similar saying: 'The greatest reward for service is the privilege of serving.' No preacher of the gospel who is worth his salt could fail to identify with these sentiments. What could be more rewarding than the privilege of declaring God's Word to a receptive congregation?

This reward is not related to our role in the Christian church. After comparing himself with Apollos and Peter, Paul wrote that each of them, with differing functions, would receive from God a reward 'according to his own labour' (1 Cor. 3:8). Surely the shut-in prayer partner is as important to the growth of a local church as the preacher in the pulpit. The reward will be revealed in glory, but the importance of these 'hidden' ministries should be acknowledged now. One recalls the lady in Bournemouth who said, 'Every time the pastor enters the pulpit I pray.' No wonder the church thrived.

Another appearance of our word is the reference in 1 Corinthians 3:14. If our work for the Lord has eternal value, we will receive our reward. The emphasis here falls on the quality of our ministry. The superficial service of gimmicks and emotional enthusiasm must certainly produce superficial spiritual life. This sort of spiritual candy-floss will melt under the scrutiny of eternity. Ours then is the task of building solidly, so the spiritual house of God will not collapse under judgement like a house of cards. For our reward is associated with the durability of our congregation. Never forget, God judges and it is he who passes out the rewards or reprimands.

God's pay-day

Do you remember your first pay-day? At sixteen I had landed a job with Priehs Department Store in the centre of our town. My humble task was sweeping the floor early in the morning and assisting in the carpet department after school. That first pay-day will remain etched on my mind until my last pay-day. It was my very own money, and I felt like a millionaire.

The Greek word *misthos* means *payment or wage for work*. The Lord instructed the apostles to expect the provision of food and drink, 'for the worker deserves his wages' (Luke 10:7). When explaining the facts of church life, Paul resurrects this principle by teaching that elders likewise deserve to be paid, and he quotes the word of the Lord: 'The worker deserves his wages' (1 Tim. 5:18). James assails greedy employers who withhold wages from their workers, because these wages withheld 'are crying out against you' (James 5:4).

In these days of precarious economic realities, it is well for employers to remember that God is the ultimate Auditor of their books. He knows when they defraud workmen of their wages, just as he knows when workmen extract payment from proprietors without producing adequate work.

A second meaning of our word is *reward for good deeds*. Here the emphasis falls not on monetary payment but on divine reward. In the Sermon on the Mount Christ encourages his disciples to face persecution with joy, 'because great is your reward in heaven' (Matt. 5:12). Later he asked, 'If you love those who love you, what reward will you get?' (Matt. 5:46). Anyone who arrogantly does '"acts of righteousness" before men, to be seen by them . . . will have no reward from your Father in heaven' (Matt. 6:1). Spiritual rewards are eternal and exclusive. To accept praise from men for spiritual work is to forfeit the right to rewards in heaven.

A friend of mine, R.T. Kendall, is writing a book on heaven. In studying for this book and writing it, he has gained a new insight into the glories of the glory. In fact, he feels that modern preachers have robbed the people of heaven's hope by retreating into an evangelical rationalism.

There is a third meaning of our word, and it is *punishment*. In the Revelation the apostle John dwells upon eternal verities. He reveals the ultimate triumph of the Christ and the final fall of the Evil One. Christians are swept along in the train of their triumphant Lord. Those who persist in sin, however, are condemned to separation from God throughout eternity. So sobering is this truth that many have denied the eternal nature of hell. They simply cannot allow themselves to believe in eternal torment. After enumerating the sins of man and the sanctity of the saints, the risen Lord declares this truth: 'Behold, I am coming soon! My reward is with me, and I will give to everyone according to what he has done' (Rev. 22:12).

Judas betrayed the Lord for thirty pieces of silver. When

he tried to reverse his action, the authorities would not hear of it. In despair Judas committed suicide, and a burial plot was purchased with the blood money. This money was called 'the reward of unrighteousness' (Acts 1:18). So punishment and reward overlap in some cases.

One form of modern literature is television and radio drama. As children we used to imitate this kind of drama by playing a game called 'cops and robbers'. In our extemporaneous spectacles, the police always triumphed and the criminals were 'shot dead' with a cap pistol or even a stick. In a sense we were giving vent to a basic principle stamped on our souls by the Creator.

The great revival preacher of America, Jonathan Edwards (1703-58) summarized this principle of divine rewards in his famous sermon: 'Sinners in the Hands of an Angry God': 'This that you have heard is the case of every one of you that are out of Christ. The world of misery, that lake of burning brimstone, is extended abroad under you. There is the dreadful pit of the glowing flames of the wrath of God; there is hell's wide gaping mouth open.'

1. Virgil, *Aeneid*, i, 461.

18.
Good example

'These things occurred as **examples***'* (1 Cor. 10:6)
'These things happened to them as **examples***'* (1 Cor. 10:11)

Although Georg Wilhelm Friedrich Hegel (1770-1831) was probably not the first to think it, he is surely the most famous proponent of the proposition: 'The only thing we learn from history is that we learn nothing from history.'

Another twist was given to the dictum by George Santayana (1863-1952), the Spanish-born American poet and philosopher. According to Santayana, 'Those who forget history are bound to repeat it.' An even more popular parody of the Hegelian axiom came from the acid-dipped pen of Irma Brombeck: 'If we would listen to history, it would stop repeating itself.'

So the gist of 1 Corinthians 10:1-13 is this secular truth: experience is a largely unproductive method of teaching. The apostle Paul here introduces the example of the 'passover generation', who were liberated from slavery in Egypt only to perish because of slavery to their own lusts.

These experiences of Israel should be an example to us, according to the apostle. The word translated 'example' is the Greek term *tupos*, and it is reflected in such English derivatives as 'type', 'typical', 'typology' and 'typography'. The root meaning of the word is seen in the English and Latin forms. 'Type' means to make an impression, and the basic Greek word *(tupos)* meant the 'mark of a stroke or blow'.

In introducing the subject, Paul asserts that the incidents of Jewish history occurred 'as examples', literally 'to make an impression' upon us (1 Cor. 10:6). The Israelites were guided through the Red Sea to show God's ability to save in trouble. Food appeared miraculously in the form of manna, to show God's providential provision for us. A rock was even split to open a refreshing flow of water to the parched pilgrims in the desert (1 Cor. 10:1-4).

Unfortunately, this did not leave much of an impression on the wanderers. Approximately three million people escaped on the first Passover night, but only two of them, Joshua and Caleb, finally arrived in the promised land. Paul implies that the majority of Corinthian Christians were scarcely more receptive to divine truth.

God gave us the Old Testament history of Israel to educate us to expect great things from him. Sadly we have missed the point, and these examples have left very little impression either on contemporary Christians or their Corinthian counterparts.

A second reference to our word *tupos* is found in this passage. 'These things happened to them [Israel] as examples.' claims Paul, 'and [they] were written down as warnings for us, on whom the fulfilment of the ages has come' (1 Cor. 10:11). In the previous passage Paul outlines some of the sins of Israel. They lived lustfully and God gave them what they wanted, a varied diet, but he punished their lust (1 Cor. 10:6). While Moses was meeting God on the summit of Sinai, Aaron led Israel in a pagan dance around a golden calf (1 Cor. 10:7). When their travels took them to Moab, they succumbed to Baal-Peor's prostitution of worship (1 Cor. 10:8), and (in round figures) between 23,000 (1 Cor. 10:8) and 24,000 (Num. 25:9) died. Furthermore, the Israelites turned their back on faithful men like Joshua and Caleb and grumbled against God. He unleashed among them a scourge of snakes (1 Cor. 10:9-10).

The inescapable implication of these scriptural object lessons is this: disobey God and he will punish you in time and eternity. The Jews' history is loaded with 'examples' *(tupoi)* to prove this. Woe to the man who treats biblical history as Henry Ford did human history when he said, 'History is bunk'!

Making a mark

Truth should always leave a mark on us, especially when it is

Bible truth. Just now the whole question of corporal punishment in school has surfaced, with a blanket condemnation of it by the European Court of Human Rights. There may be debate on whether or not teachers should use a cane or even a hand to punish their pupils. (Though, corporal punishment marked my attitude for good more than it marked my anatomy for evil.) Although one debates corporal punishment, no one denies that schools should make an impression on their pupils.

The word *tupos* speaks of an impression being made. It is translated, as already seen, as *'example'*. The apostle Paul urged his protégé Timothy to be an 'example for the believers' (1 Tim. 4:12). Paul saw it as his responsibility to be an example to Christians (Phil. 3:17). Churches were to be an example to the world around them (1 Thess. 1:7).

In the United States I have a much-valued friend and elder brother in the ministry. He possesses a magnificent library of several thousand theological works. On the wall is a large montage of preachers' pictures. These are the men to whom he owes much. Our primary example is, of course, the Lord, but never let us forget men and women of God whose example has left a mark on us.

A second translation of our word *tupos* is *'pattern'*. Roman Christians were commended by the hitherto absent apostle because they 'whole-heartedly obeyed the form' (pattern) 'of teaching to which' they were entrusted (Rom. 6:17). Undoubtedly they had taken in the apostles' teaching during early days in Jerusalem, and now they continued in this truth as it was expanded in epistles.

Titus was instructed by the apostle Paul to set Cretian Christians 'an example' *(tupos)* 'by doing what is good' (Titus 2:7). Christian leaders in every circumstance and church are commissioned to be exemplary in their lives. Here, too, the basic meaning of our word shines through. The good works of Christian leaders should leave an impression on Christians and non-Christians alike.

The idea here is that of a pattern. When my wife sews a dress, she sticks very close to the pattern. As she cuts out the material, much time and effort are taken to ensure that the cloth is cut in conformity with both the weave of the material and the demands of the pattern. Christians need a pattern of faith, a biblical basis of doctrine to which they agree. They also require a pattern of ethics in an age when immorality runs rampant, like a river in full flood. The destruction wrought by this immoral inundation far surpasses any mere natural disaster known to man.

A third translation of our word is predictable; it is *type*. The New Testament sometimes imputes typological meaning to Old Testament institutions or people. For instance, Adam is seen as 'a pattern' *(tupos)* 'of the one to come' (Rom. 5:14). There are obvious and vast discrepancies between Adam and Christ. However, under the Holy Spirit's inspiration the apostle Paul compares the first Adam with the last Adam. Their similarity is seen in terms of universal and unique impact on human history. Adam plunged his progeny into sin, while Christ imparts to Christians righteousness.

Another type is found in Hebrews 8:5, where the Jews were instructed to erect a tabernacle according to the 'pattern shown you on the mountain'. This architectural pattern was in turn a pattern of the heavenly sanctuary.

Now typology is traditional. In years gone by earnest preachers peered into the Bible and saw things which were hidden from human view, types which sometimes existed only in the eye of the beholder. Most expositors avoid typology today. However, we must be careful not to dump out the baby with the bath water, or to throw out all types with the tub of typology. Some types, like the ones mentioned above, are biblical, and the New Testament must be our criterion to distinguish the true from the fantastic.

The real meaning of our word *tupos* is profoundly simple. The pattern, example and type of Old Testament experience and truth must be taken seriously and applied spiritually in our lives. Otherwise, we, like Hegel and his friends, will only learn from history that we learn nothing from it.

19.
Take part

'**Participation** *in the blood of Christ'* (1 Cor. 10:16)
'**Participate** *in the altar'* (1 Cor. 10:18)
'**Participants** *with demons'* (1 Cor. 10:20)

Taking part is a modern adaptation of the old-fashioned word
'fellowship'. 'Fellowship' is much used and much abused.
Some see it in the shape of a teacup. To them fellowship is a
hot cup of milky tea liberally laced with sugar. A biscuit adds
to the lavishness of the 'fellowship'. Whether or not people
actually take part in each other's lives is irrelevant.

Others view fellowship as a religious meeting, a service.
Birds of a feather flock together, on time, and sit in a more
or less comatose state for upwards of an hour. At the end
they all fly back to their little box houses and claim they
have enjoyed fellowship.

A third view of fellowship is discussion. This much-flaunted
fad of the seventies and eighties presupposes that a free-
ranging discussion deepens spiritual life. The ruthlessness of
this view is seen when one considers the inarticulate who are
temperamentally unsuited to take part in such a verbal free-
for-all. For them it is certainly not a meaningful meeting of
persons.

Our Greek word is a trendy slogan, *koinonia.* Bauer's
Greek-English Lexicon of the New Testament translates this
word with a raft of synonyms: association, communion,
fellowship, close relationship, generosity, participation and
even sharing. In its various forms, the word crops up about
forty times in the New Testament, and eight of these uses
appear in the Corinthian letters.

In the above-quoted passage (1 Cor. 10) the word is translated by the New International Version as 'participation'. The
act of communion or the Lord's Table is described as 'participation in the blood of Christ . . . participation in the body

of Christ' (1 Cor. 10:16). When Christians meet to observe the Lord's Supper, there is personal participation in Christ. This is primarily a spiritual act, in which we declare that we have benefited by faith from the sacrifice of Christ. It is a personal occasion in which we say symbolically, 'Christ died to atone for my sin.' In this sense we participate in the benefits of the atonement. (Of course, the communion elements carry no mystical or magical spiritual power in themselves, as the Roman Catholics teach.)

Paul explained this by contrast. He showed that those who feasted in idolatrous temples actually participated in idolatry (1 Cor. 10:20). This aspect of religious commitment is seen in honest Marxists, who regard their philosophy in terms of religion. Some even speak of participation in the spirit of Lenin or Marx.

A by-product of this Pauline teaching is seen in the later Corinthian letter. 'Light and darkness' have nothing in common (2 Cor. 6:14). Obviously this does not refer to the abstract mixture of light and darkness, but rather to the association of the spiritually enlightened with the spiritually blind.

Yet another aspect of our word is seen in 2 Corinthians 8:4, where financial assistance to starving saints in Judea is described as 'sharing' (fellowshipping) 'in this service to the saints'. Real fellowship involves giving, and this is especially appropriate when other Christians are in need. Later on, Paul thanks the Corinthian Christians for their 'generosity in sharing' (fellowshipping) 'with them and with everyone else' (2 Cor. 9:13). In our day we hide behind the social services and pretend ignorance of human need. Early Christians opened their eyes and their purses more readily.

When the apostle concluded his letter to the Corinthians, he did so with a benediction which we often repeat. It, too, contains our word: 'May the grace of the Lord Jesus Christ, and the love of God, and the fellowship of the Holy Spirit be with you all' (2 Cor. 13:14).

Fair shares

Sharing is bigger than words. In our day we are often urged

to 'share some prayer requests' or 'share our testimony'. A syrupy sentimentality surrounds the word 'sharing'. In certain circles a sweater-clad teddy-bear of a preacher stands up and tells the group: 'I'm just going to share a few thoughts with you.' 'Sharing' is a euphemism, an embarrassed excuse for preaching used by those who have not much to say.

In the New Testament 'sharing' (*koinonia*, fellowship) was a word for hard-headed and hot-hearted involvement. They were first of all *involved with God*. The apostle John spoke of 'fellowship with the Father and with his Son, Jesus Christ' (1 John 1:3). This fellowship extended to identification with Christ's resurrection power, crucifixion sufferings and humiliating death (Phil. 3:10). There was a depth of involvement with God that spurned superficiality. For first-century Christians, 'fellowship' with God meant 'disfellowship' with every worldly association. In our day the barrier between believers and the world is so blurred that we can hardly tell where the church leaves off and the social club begins.

Another aspect of our word is *involvement in the church*. One of the primary characteristics of the Jerusalem church was 'fellowship' (Acts 2:42). This was a continual experience, as was apostolic teaching, breaking of bread and prayer. No room existed for mere hangers-on, and these early Christians were expected to exercise complete commitment.

Today every church has 'fellow travellers'. Something in the church attracts them, so they drift into the services. Depending on the degree of attraction, they may be more or less faithful at worship. Never do they commit themselves to membership or responsibility. Together they comprise a pitiful platoon of evangelical tramps who move around like locusts stripping the blessing from fellowships. The Bible makes involvement an indispensable element of Christian life.

A third use of our word *koinonia* is *involvement in giving*. To the Romans Paul held up the example of Macedonians and Greeks who 'were pleased to make a contribution' (share) 'for the poor among the saints in Jerusalem' (Rom. 15:26). Christians who benefit from teaching are instructed to 'share all good things' with their instructor (Gal. 6:6). In a parting word, the writer of Hebrews gives the same teaching: 'Do not

forget to do good and to share with others, for with such
sacrifices God is pleased' (Heb. 13:16).

Christian giving is not optional but essential. Real fellowship
means the sharing of our goods with those in need. To hoard
our wealth and resist the appeal of brothers and sisters in
need is to fly in the face of biblical revelation.

As a boy I remember hearing a big, round, jolly man speak.
His name was R.G. LeTourneau (1888-1969) who made
millions manufacturing earth-moving machinery. He urged us
as young people to give to the Lord's work. In fact, LeTourneau gave 90% of his earnings to the Lord and lived on the
remaining tithe. When he died his wealth was stored up in
heaven.

There is no escaping the need to be involved. Any Christian
who hides in a pew and tries to pretend he is uninvolved is a
candidate for spiritual shipwreck.

20.
Permissible practices

'"Everything is **permissible** *" — but not everything is beneficial. "Everything is* **permissible** *" — but not everything is constructive'* (1 Cor. 10:23)

Right and wrong are perennially practical puzzlers. 'One may go wrong in many different ways,' decided Aristotle (384-322 B.C.), 'but right only in one.' Cato the Elder (234-149 B.C.) echoed the sentiment when he said, 'I prefer to do right and get no thanks, rather than do wrong and get no punishment.'

Few would take issue with this analysis of ethics, but most would question the definition of right and wrong. At any given time there are current issues of right and wrong. In our day there seethe such lively subjects as abortion, euthanasia, nuclear disarmament, civil rights — and the list is almost endless.

When one seeks for a Christian ethic, there are several levels of authority to be considered. First, there are the clear biblical commands, which sort out issues that are clearly black or white. Second, there are matters of civic law which likewise limit our ethical considerations. Third, traditional Christian practice places some further items out of bounds. Finally, there are many issues which are left to Christian conscience for a decision.

The word translated 'permissible' in 1 Corinthians 10:23 is an impersonal Greek verb, *existi*, and it is probably related through the Latin *existere* to our word 'exist'. The Greek word goes beyond mere existence (what is) and extends to a definition of what is 'permitted, possible, or proper'. This possibility is defined either by law, or nature or even by accepted custom. Lest explanation fuel confusion, we shall illustrate the word only as it occurs in the New Testament.

In 1 Corinthians it is used only in one formula. 'Everything is permissible' but not everything is beneficial or constructive (1 Cor. 10:23). The ethical decision is not purely a personal decision. It relates also to the church at large. So Christians cannot pervert privilege to cause the spiritual suffering of another. Charles Simmons summed it up in these words: 'No man has the right to do as he pleases, except when he pleases to do right.' Paul explains ethical decisions by relating them to other people. Does my action benefit another person and build up that person?

The other use of our word in 1 Corinthians is a similar axiom: '"Everything is permissible for me" — but not everything is beneficial. "Everything is permissible for me " — but I will not be mastered by anything' (1 Cor. 6:12). Paul here ruled out any habit which usurped control over his conscience. In our day addiction is a major problem, with the number of alcohol and drug addicts growing daily. Even Christians come under the control of addiction, and it is Paul's contention here that this is 'not permissible'. No habit should steal the lordship which belongs to Christ alone.

Crossing over into the other Corinthian letter, we find one further appearance of our word. Here Paul describes his *ecstatic* (literally, 'out of place') experience. In an apparently autobiographical statement, Paul says, 'He heard inexpressible things, things that man is not permitted' *(existi)* 'to tell' (2 Cor. 12:4). What Paul heard was so overwhelming that it burst the bounds of human finiteness. He had fathomed something of the unfathomable. To put this in words was impossible, even to the Holy Spirit-inspired mind of the apostle. Here the limit was simply the limits of language which could not contain such spiritual truth.

Our word, then, is an elastic word. It can refer to limits imposed by Christian ethics and calculated to edify the church. On the other hand, it can refer to the limits of created being beyond which no mortal can move.

Beyond the pale

In the days before Cromwell, English residents in Ireland lived a very precarious life. Having imposed imperial rule on the Irish, English authorities thought it politic to limit the movement of their functionaries to the immediate environs of Dublin. To wander outside this relatively safe sphere of activity was to go 'beyond the pale'. The phrase also applied to a sphere of English sovereignty around Calais during the period of English domination, 1347-1558.

Our word *existi* speaks of those matters which are ethically 'beyond the pale'. First, the word was misapplied by the *Pharisees*. When the disciples ate grain in the field on the sabbath, the Pharisees pounced. 'Look!' they lashed out at Jesus, 'Your disciples are doing what is *unlawful* on the Sabbath' (Matt. 12:2). Jesus picked them up on the word *existi*, when he answered, 'It is lawful' *(existi)* 'to do good on the Sabbath' (Matt. 12:12).

In the hands of the Pharisees the Mosaic law had been twisted out of all scriptural shape. God gave the law as a sheltering boundary; the Pharisees turned it into an imprisoning fetter. When God gave the law it was intended to create order out of social chaos, but the Pharisees made the law a trap to ensnare people, especially the Lord Jesus Christ.

A second use of our word is in the mouth of *preachers*. The fearless forerunner of Messiah, John the Baptist, appeared before the unprincipled Herod and said, 'It is not lawful' *(existi)* 'for you to have' your brother's wife (Matt. 14:4). Here is courageous application of moral truth, which has great relevance in our relativistic and immoral age. In fact, most ministers must make similar statements, but few will lose their heads as literally as John did. In this case 'not lawful' is traced back to essential biblical law.

When the apostle Paul used the phrase, he referred back to Roman law. 'Is it *legal*', he asked the Roman commander, 'for you to flog a Roman citizen who hasn't even been found guilty?' (Acts 22:25.) Here the apostle took advantage of law, just as Christians under totalitarian governments still claim legal rights. Alas, they usually are severely restricted in the exercise of those rights.

One final expression of our word is found in the *Lord's* mouth. King David had during his days as a refugee entered the sacred precincts and procured sacramental bread to eat, bread 'which *is lawful only* for priests to eat' (Mark 2:26). The abiding lesson which Christ drew from this incident is this: 'The Sabbath was made for man, not man for the Sabbath' (Mark 2:27). Christ is Lord of the sabbath as well as every other day in the week.

When we ask, 'Is it lawful?' or 'Is it permissible?' we must focus first on the criterion by which all such questions are judged. Of course, that criterion is the biblical revelation of the Lord. Many issues are completely clear, and about these there is no question. It is the large and shifting scale of questionable practices which makes us prayerfully determine our position. In 1 Corinthians 10:23-33 there are three most helpful principles to guide us in determining what is permissible. First, is it constructive and encouraging to Christian growth? (1 Cor. 10:23-24.) Second, is it right and not hurtful to another Christian? (1 Cor. 10:25-30.) Third, does it glorify God and and point people to the living Lord of the church? (1 Cor. 10:31-33.)

21.
It's a shame!

'Shame on you!' mothers used to say to disobedient offspring. In other words, your behaviour is not proper; it is shameful, it dishonours child and parent. Thankfully this reprimand usually corrected the child, and the mini-man or woman grew to be a more or less civilized citizen.

Shame can be a helpful instrument in training a child, but it can also be totally devastating. One thinks of the Japanese custom of 'hara-kiri'. When a Samurai warrior had been dishonoured, the only remaining means of restoring his honour was suicide. There followed a ghastly ceremony of disembowelment. Surely this is too high a price for honour!

In our culture shame has a lower price-tag. Some years ago a neighbour deserted his wife for another woman. The man was cultured and indeed he was a professional musician. When he realized that the neighbours knew about his 'shameful' behaviour, he simply moved house. However, his shame did cost him dearly, for it meant separation from his wife and a loving family.

The Greek word which is translated 'dishonour' in our 1 Corinthians text is *kataischuno*. In other passages it is rendered as 'shame', 'embarrassment', 'humiliation' or even 'modesty'.

The reference to *kataischuno* (1 Cor. 11:4-5) is rather clouded in obscurity, for it speaks of 'dishonouring' one's head. The idea seems to be that a head-covering for women was customary in ancient Greece among Christians. Actually it was long hair covered by a veil. To pray without the long hair and covering veil was an affront to accepted customs of modesty, because only loose women cut their hair and went without the veil.

By the same token, Greek Christian men, indeed, all male Christians, had broken with the Jewish custom of praying with the head covered. Therefore to cover the head for prayer was 'dishonouring' to a man. There is also a Greek word-play here. For the man is uniquely under the headship of Christ, and to pray with the head covered is to dishonour his Head, Christ (1 Cor. 11:3-4).

It is important to ascertain what this passage does *not* teach. First, it does not teach the superiority of one sex over another, for we all are alike responsible to God (Gal. 3:28). Second, it does not teach the necessity of wearing decorative hats. The New Testament head-covering was a veil over the whole *head* including and especially the face. Third, it does not reflect an absolute command. The veil was a sign of submission by the woman to her husband, and today there are other signs of submission, such as a wedding ring, or bearing the husband's surname.

There are several other occurrences of our word *kataischuno* in the Corinthian correspondence. The Lord has chosen weak and unimpressive people to 'shame' the great of this world (1 Cor. 1:27). Paul is a walking illustration of this principle, and he rejoiced that his claims concerning Corinthian Christians were justified. He commended them by writing, 'You have not embarrassed' *(shamed)* 'me' (2 Cor. 7:14). Their generosity towards Christians in need was exemplary, so Paul was gratified and he was not 'ashamed of having been so confident' concerning them (2 Cor. 9:4). This emboldened Paul to praise the Corinthians for their faithfulness and to thank God for 'the authority the Lord gave us for building you up rather than pulling you down'. Then the apostle adds, 'I will not be ashamed of it' (2 Cor. 10:8).

There is a subtle exchange in the Christian revelation. What is incomprehensible and embarrassing to the world is not a shame to Christians. For instance, in the world weak people are walked over, but in Christ the meek become mighty. In the world wealthy people are sought after, but in Christ wealth can become a great snare. In the world intellectual brilliance spawns superiority, but Christians see simplicity as a virtue.

Thus 'shame' and 'dishonour' are double-edged verities. Godly shame over sin is like pain, a God-given warning sign to aid healing. When men dishonour a Christian and attempt to shame him, they inadvertently elevate him to glory with God.

Who has a red face?

When I was a teenager, the slightest embarrassment ignited a blush in my face. The first morning at college I gingerly carried my breakfast tray to the table. As I started to take the food off the tray a bowl of porridge tipped over, cascading down my clothing and the furniture. Needless to say, my face burned with a scarlet glow.

The above illustration from personal experience is morally neutral, but shame usually has a moral meaning in the Scriptures. There are two elementary truths relating to this. First, *some should be ashamed.*

On a certain sabbath Jesus straightened up a crippled woman, and the religious spectators pounced on him. The Lord reasoned that even a farm animal could be freed on the sabbath, and certainly it was right to free this sufferer. When he finished 'all his opponents were *humiliated*' (Luke 13:17). Those who oppose the Lord should be put to shame, and openly, too.

When loose-tongued tyrants taunt Christians, they will be silenced by the saints' godly lives. Christian witness in this case serves an apologetic purpose, 'so that those who speak maliciously against your good behaviour in Christ may be ashamed of their slander' (1 Peter 3:16). Those who heap abuse on a Christian should be publicly shamed by the Christian's consistent life and word. One sees this in the Soviet Union where the mildest of Christians sometimes become an acute embarrassment to the atheistic authorities. One recalls here the Siberian Seven, who sought refuge in the United States Embassy.

But there are also some who *shall never be put to shame.* In the Septuagint Greek Old Testament our word occurs in

Psalm 119:31. There the psalmist rejoices, 'I hold fast to your statutes, O Lord; do not let me be put to shame.'

The same idea finds an echo in the New Testament. 'Hope does not *disappoint*' (shame) 'us, because God has poured out his love into our hearts by the Holy Spirit, whom he has given us' (Rom. 5:5). We are not ashamed of our sinful past, because through God's regenerating work that past is truly put behind us.

When describing Christ as the Rock, the apostle adds a quotation from Isaiah 28:16, that 'The one who trusts in him will never be put to shame' (Rom. 9:33). The great guarantee against being ashamed in eternity is our trust in the Lord. It is not our fidelity but his firmness which guards us against shame. One thinks of the courageous Christians who have acted on this confidence. When William Carey (1761-1834) embarked for India, it was his unlimited reliance on the Lord which nerved him to overcome mountainous obstacles in establishing his great work at Serampore. Carey was convinced that God would not let him slip into shame.

Charles Wesley (1707-88) summarized Christian confidence when he wrote the little rhyme we love to sing:

> Faith, mighty faith, the promise sees
> And looks to that alone,
> Laughs at impossibilities
> And cries: It shall be done.

22.
Heresies and schisms

'There are **divisions***' (schisms) 'among you'* (1 Cor. 11:18)
*'***Differences***' (heresies) 'among you'* (1 Cor. 11:19)

Heresy has hampered the progress of the gospel from the first. Before the New Testament was completed the Gnostics were gnawing away at the deity of Christ and sovereign salvation. During the first four centuries heretics nibbled away at the biblical teaching concerning Christ. Arians attacked his deity, while the Nestorians negated his humanity.

During the Dark Ages heresy harried the church as Roman Catholic culture became confused with biblical Christianity. Salvation was taken hostage to papal privilege. By the dawn of the sixteenth century one could hear the Vatican money collector Johann Tetzel (about 1465-1519) sing, 'When the money clinks into the box, the sinner is freed from sin.' Such a crass commercial concept of salvation became a springboard for the Reformation.

Later the target of heresy became the Bible. Human reason was elevated through the Enlightenment to be the criterion of truth. When the Bible and reason conflict, it was presumed that the Scriptures were false. This produced the theology of men like Rudolf Bultmann (1884-1976), who sought to strip the Bible of 'myth' and in doing so did away with miracles.

In our consideration we take two words. The first word is *schisma*, and it is transliterated into our English word 'schism'. It springs from the Greek verb *schizo*, 'to split, divide, separate or tear asunder'. One sees it in the English word 'schizophrenic' — one with 'divided' *(schizo)* 'thinking' *(phren)*.

In modern ecclesiastical language, a 'schism' means a division in the church. Paul uses this word frequently in 1 Corinthians. In 1 Corinthians 1:10 he pleaded with the Christians to 'agree with one another so that there may be no divisions' (schisms) 'among you and that you may be perfectly united in mind and thought'. When dealing with the matter of spiritual gifts, Paul again emphasized this. 'There should be no division' (schism) 'in the body,' he admonished (1 Cor. 12:25).

'Schism is a practical heresy,' wrote Archbishop Richard Trench (1807-86), 'heresy is a theoretical schism.' In 1 Corinthians 11:19 Paul substantiates Trench's teaching, by asserting that 'differences' (heresies) underlie the schisms in verse 18. Calvin called these heresies 'a magnet to attract the unsound and unsettled mind'.[1]

The Greek word for 'heresy' is *hairesis*. In other words, here, too, we have an English transliteration, the English spelling of a Greek word. The Greek root means 'to choose or select'. Heretics select one teaching and blow it up out of proportion to the rest of biblical revelation and doctrine. For instance, the Mormons elevate biblical injunctions to holy living and make obedience to church instruction a requirement for salvation. In Mormon literature salvation by grace is perverted into a concept of salvation by the aid of human effort. Heresy is usually a biblical doctrine which has grown grotesque by human emphasis, a cancer cell which grows too fast and results in death.

So schism and heresy are Siamese twins. Without heresy there is seldom schism, and schism fuels the heretical teaching which spawned it. These Siamese twins were a blot on the worship of the Corinthian Christians, and they are a constant threat today, too.

Why churches split

Schism is a common phenomenon in evangelical circles. When I was young in the faith and still studying for the ministry, my home church endured a traumatic division. The tentacles of trouble reached into many families, and their poisonous power lasted long after the splinter fellowship was founded.

Schism and heresy are seen throughout the Scriptures. First, we shall survey briefly the word *schism*. It is used *literally to describe a violent dividing*. When Jesus died on the cross, the 'curtain of the temple was torn' *(schizo)* 'from top to bottom. The earth shook and the rocks split' *(schizo)* (Matt. 27:51). The emphasis falls both on the dividing and the violent nature of the act.

In an *abstract sense*, the same two elements occur. During Christ's day, 'the people were divided' *(schizo)* 'because of Jesus' (John 7:43). The preaching of Paul and Barnabas at Iconium had the effect that 'the people of the city were divided' *(schizo)*; 'some sided with the Jews, others with the apostles' (Acts 14:4).

Later, of course, division invaded the church. The Corinthian church was the primary example of this sad split. Not only were the Christians divided according to loyalty to leaders, but also according to various doctrinal and practical perversions.

Many modern cultic movements trace their beginnings to schism in biblical churches. Sun Myung Moon left the normally orthodox Presbyterian Church of Korea to form his bizarre personality cult. Two centuries ago Unitarians renounced belief in the Trinity and abandoned the American Episcopal Church and Congregational Church. Last century William Miller (1782-1849) rejected his Baptist background and invented the Adventist movement in about 1831.

From the above-mentioned schisms, one can easily see the source in our second word, *heresy*. Paul warned the Galatians about this. 'Factions' (literally 'heresies'), according to the concerned apostle, are 'acts of the sinful nature' (Gal. 5:19-20).

The apostle Peter was even more scathing in his attack. 'False prophets ... will secretly introduce destructive heresies,' he wrote, 'even denying the sovereign Lord who bought them — bringing swift destruction on themselves' (2 Peter 2:1). It is interesting to note that Peter identifies these false prophets as Christians bought by the Lord, but he also warns them of spiritual bankruptcy comparable to Paul's threat of spiritual shipwreck (1 Tim. 1:19).

In our day such heresy centres upon the doctrine of salvation. Many cults teach either explicitly or implicitly that we are saved by grace through faith *plus* good works or religious conformity, or some such thing. One thinks here of the Mormons, Moonies, Hare Krishna, or even the Seventh Day Adventists. (Admittedly, the heresy is more implicit than explicit in some of these cults.)

Despite the disclaimers of charismatic Catholics and the friendly character of Pope John Paul II, one sees a continuing heretical tendency in Roman Catholicism. Salvation is still mediated mainly through the sacraments of the church, especially the mass. Prayer is made through the Virgin Mary, in direct contrast to the instruction of Jesus that we ask the Father in the Lord's name (John 16:24).

The answer to schism and heresy is not a doctrinal crusade to eradicate false teaching, but rather a solid commitment to biblical doctrine and declaration. The greatest antidote to counterfeit money is real money, and the corrective for false doctrine is the patient teaching of true doctrine.

Samuel J. Stone (1839-1900) summarized this truth in his famous hymn:

> By schisms rent asunder, by heresies distressed;
> Yet saints their watch are keeping,
> Their cry goes up, How long?
> And soon the night of weeping
> Shall be the morn of song.

1. *Calvin's Commentaries*, Baker, vol.20, pages 366-7.

23.
Sovereign Spirit

'No one . . . speaking by the **Spirit** *of God says, "Jesus be
cursed", and no one can say, "Jesus is Lord", except by
the Holy* **Spirit***'* (1 Cor. 12:3)

No subject has generated more heat in the mid-twentieth
century than that of the Holy Spirit. He has become the
centre of a theological tornado which has left division and
destruction everywhere.

Dorothy Sayers (1893-1957) expressed this rather cynical
view of opinion about the Holy Spirit. 'There are those who
worship the Father, the Son and the Virgin Mary,' she mused,
'those who believe in the Father, the Son and the Holy
Scriptures; those who found their faith on the Father, the
Son and the Church; and there are even those who seem to
derive their spiritual power from the Father, the Son and the
minister!'

If Dorothy Sayers' trinitarian turn-about is accurate, it is
surely lamentable. No biblical believer could opt for any
option except the biblical trinity which properly places the
Holy Spirit. He is personal (no mere force), powerful (no
insipid emotion), and present (no possession of the particularly
pious).

The word translated 'Spirit' in the New Testament is
pneuma. It is seen in such words as *pneuma*tic (driven by air
pressure), *pneum*onia (the infection of the lungs), and *pneumo*-
graph (an instrument to measure breathing). The root word
pneuma appears 377 times in the New Testament and eleven
times in 1 Corinthians 12 alone. It is 1 Corinthians which we
shall focus upon in this brief chapter. There the Holy Spirit is
portrayed in living detail. First, he is seen as the *saving Spirit*.
Without his presence no one can respond to the lordship of
Jesus Christ. Only by the Holy Spirit can one see the truth
that Jesus of history is the Lord of eternity. Anyone who

curses Christ has no relationship to the Holy Spirit (1 Cor.
12:3).

This saving aspect of the Holy Spirit's work teaches some
practical lessons. You cannot discover the lordship of Christ
without the Holy Spirit; he *alone* opens eyes, convicts conscience and produces repentance and faith. Furthermore, you
cannot have the Holy Spirit and live as you wish: the Holy
Spirit is grieved and quenched when he shares the human
breast with sin. Finally, you cannot have the Spirit and
deny the Scripture: he has inspired and now illumines the
Scriptures.

There is a second function of the Holy Spirit in 1 Corinthians 12:4-9. Here he is seen as the *serving Spirit*. He equips
Christians to minister to one another and thus construct the
church of Christ. A list of gifts is found in verses 8-10, and
some will be discussed when we consider 1 Corinthians 14.
However, several foundational truths emerge from the twelfth
chapter of 1 Corinthians.

Each believer has at least one gift (v.7). Each gift supports
the church as a Christian community (v.7). Each person is
enjoined to work with his or her gift. Spiritual gifts are not
ornaments on a shelf but tools on a work-bench (vv.6, 10).

The church is compared to a human body (1 Cor. 12:12).
The body is animated by the nervous system. There is one
brain-driven nervous system which animates the ear to hear,
the eye to see, the nose to sniff and the fingers to feel. The
organs are vastly diverse, but the moving force is one. Christians
are likewise very different, but the Life-Giver is the Holy
Spirit.

A third truth about the Holy Spirit is also here. He is the
sovereign Spirit. He gives gifts to his people, 'just as he determines' (1 Cor. 12:11). The unity of the Spirit permeates
1 Corinthians 12. Four times there appears the phrase, 'the
same Spirit' (1 Cor. 12:4, 8, 9, 11).

His sovereignty unifies all Spirit-indwelt people in the world
and in eternity. Differences are on the surface. Nationalities,
even in time of war, are superficial. (One recalls the touching
incident of German and Allied forces during the Great War
singing Christmas carols across the war-torn turf of France.)

Never let us forget, however, that spiritual unity only occurs where the Holy Spirit is resident and where Christ is really Lord.

The secret of true spirituality

Ours is a day of instant gratification. I drink coffee often, and even a culinary incompetent like me can make instant coffee by boiling water and pouring it over the granules. But true spirituality is not achieved instantly or easily. Only the Holy Spirit can make man spiritual. Thus we view the Spirit from various aspects.

First, He is *God's Spirit* (1 Peter 4:14). All the attributes of God are present in the Holy Spirit. He is everywhere to energize Christians. He knows everything and comforts battered believers. He can do anything and thus empowers our feeble efforts. All power is his, so he tolerates no resistance. The Holy Spirit is compared by Christ to the wind. He is not a gentle breeze but a powerful storm.

Second, he is the *Spirit of truth*. The Lord promised, 'He will guide you into all truth' (John 16:13). No error can stand before the blazing light of the Spirit's truth. When our spiritual leaders go to exercise spiritual discipline, the Spirit guides them into true discernment of the spiritual condition of the needy brother or sister.

Third, he is the *Holy Spirit*. No less than eighty times in the New Testament the Spirit is named the 'Holy Spirit'. This means that he is totally separate ('holy' means 'separate') from all sin. He hails from eternity and is not fenced in by time. When he invades time, he does so to bless and benefit the people of God. United with us by faith, he does not compromise his holiness, but rather works to make us holy.

Fourth, he is also the *revealing Spirit*. According to 2 Peter 1:21, 'Prophecy never had its origin in the will of man, but men spoke from God as they were carried along by the Holy Spirit.' Our Bible, both the Old and New Testaments, was revealed by the Holy Spirit. But he also opens eyes today to the truth of the Word of God. Recently I ministered to Royal

Navy personnel. Several new Christians expressed wonder. 'Why was I so blind for so long to the truth of the gospel?' they exclaimed. The answer is, of course, that they only could see gospel truth when the Holy Spirit opened their eyes.

Fifth, he is a *guiding Spirit*. When he arrived in Europe, the apostle Paul knew that he had been 'kept by the Holy Spirit from preaching the Word in the province of Asia' (Acts 16:6). Today, too, the Holy Spirit still leads men and women as they serve Him. The growing number of keen young ministers and missionaries demonstrates the dimensions of the Spirit's stimulus to service.

Finally, he is a *sensitive Spirit*. Sin in a Christian's life stops the working of the Holy Spirit: it grieves 'the Holy Spirit of God' (Eph. 4:30). News reached me recently of a pastor in America who had departed from the ways of truth and entered upon an immoral relationship. The grief this caused to his congregation was small in comparison with the awesome affront against the blessed Holy Spirit of God.

The Holy Spirit of God is not an optional extra in the Christian life. He is the Christian life. This is why we often conclude our worship with this prayer:

> May the grace of the Lord Jesus Christ,
> and the love of God,
> and the fellowship of the Holy Spirit
> be with you all (2 Cor. 13:14).

24.
Believers' baptisms

'All **baptized** *by one Spirit into one body'* (1 Cor. 12:13)

Once I was visiting the office of the Slavic Mission in Stockholm. My friend, the general secretary, invited me to view some rather remarkable amateur film. It was flickering and rather inadequately lit, but the event was electrifying. It was a clandestine baptismal service in a Russian river. The dynamism of this demonstration of faith was unforgettable. One by one the believers strode into the river and confessed their faith by baptism.

The word 'baptism' is a transliteration, a Greek word spelled with English letters. The Greek verb is *baptizo*, and it means to plunge into water or immerse. In the verb form it occurs seventy-four times in the New Testament.

In 1 Corinthians 12:13, the word is applied to Spirit baptism. The Christian is plunged into the Holy Spirit and thus introduced into the body of Christ, the church. This is not the prerogative of a privileged class of Christians. Some think of 'Spirit baptism' as the elective experience of élite Christians. It is about as available as eating artichoke hearts. Theoretically it is possible, but practically it is improbable. No, the New Testament portrays Spirit baptism as the common property of all believers.

Our word, *baptizo*, appears in several Corinthian contexts. When combatting the cliques at Corinth, Paul indicated that some sought glory by association with a certain baptizer. For that very reason Paul baptized only Crispus and Gaius (1 Cor. 1:13-17). Paul's commission centred on evangelism, not baptism. Baptism by a special person does not convey special spiritual privilege, contrary to presumption. (During his 1982 visit to Britain, Pope John Paul II baptized a representative group of new Catholics. One wondered whether his baptism of young people and adults was an attempt to avoid the thorny issue of infant baptism. Nevertheless, I am sure the baptismal candidates will attach special significance to their baptism at the hand of the gentle Polish pope.)

Another use of our word *baptizo* is the cryptic statement: 'They all were baptized into Moses in the cloud and in the sea' (1 Cor. 10:2). Here the idea seems to be that baptism is a commitment to follow one leader. Its initiatory aspect is seen here, because the Jews were initiated into the leadership of Moses.

A further, problematical, use of the word *baptizo* is found in the great resurrection chapter, 1 Corinthians 15. There Paul argues the truth of resurrection by referring to those 'who are baptized for the dead'. 'If the dead are not raised,' Paul puzzles, 'why are people baptized for them?' (1 Cor. 15:29.) Soon after our marriage, my wife sprang this tough text on me. Twenty-five years of study have intervened, and I am still uncertain about its meaning. It would seem to refer, however, to the practice of living Christians being baptized in the name of (Greek *hyper*, 'in behalf of' or 'for the sake of') deceased believers who had not been baptized prior to their death. This practice has been revived and raised to become a cardinal doctrine by Mormonism.

The subject of baptism is treated most unusually in 1 Corinthians. Three problems are presented: inordinate attachment to one baptizer (1:13-17), Israel's commitment to Moses (10:2) and baptism on behalf of the dead (15:29). The problems do not, however, obscure the blessed truth of Spirit baptism as portrayed in 1 Corinthians 12:13.

How much water?

'The Church down the centuries has been sharply divided both as to the mode and as to the rightful recipients of baptism,' according to the evangelical ecumenist Gilbert Kirby.[1] Finally Kirby boiled down baptism to two essential elements: 'the use of water and the invoking of the name of the Triune God'. (A friend dismissed the book as 'Fences I have sat upon,' and Kirby would not necessarily disagree with this diagnosis.)

Actually baptism has five meanings in the New Testament. First, it refers to ancient Jewish *ceremonial washings*. Pharisees 'give their hands a ceremonial washing' (Mark 7:4-5). The writer of the book of Hebrews also refers to 'food and drink and various ceremonial washings' *(baptismos)* (Heb. 9:10). Under the grace economy of God, these ceremonial washings have no other meaning than history. Practically, they were often erroneously used as substitutes for saving grace.

A second use of *baptizo* is *pre-Christian baptism*. John the Baptizer baptized hundreds of Jews as a sign of repentance (Matt. 3:6; John 1:25). This baptism was preliminary and inadequate. Thus converts to Christ required baptism again in the name of Christ (Acts 19:3-5).

Pre-Christian baptisms were good as far as they went. They represented obedience to light received, but further light required further obedience. This principle is seen when one who has undergone infant baptism becomes aware of the need for believers' baptism.

A third baptism is true *Christian baptism*. Jesus instructed his disciples to travel world-wide making disciples as they went. The commitment of discipleship precedes the act of baptism, which marks the initiation into a commitment to trinitarian belief. Disciples are baptized in the 'name' (singular) 'of the Father and of the Son and of the Holy Spirit' (Matt. 28:19).

The biblical order is always repentance and faith followed by baptism. Peter proclaimed this at Pentecost (Acts 2:38). The evangelist Philip pursued the same practice at Samaria (Acts 8:12) and also in his encounter with the Ethiopian treasurer (Acts 8:36-38).

No act so vividly proclaims the gospel as does believers' baptism. The impressive public confession of Christ causes even the most resistant reprobate to think seriously about the gospel message. Frequently the Lord uses baptism to persuade the unbeliever.

A fourth biblical baptism is *Spirit baptism*. John the Baptizer proclaimed that Christ would baptize us 'with the Holy Spirit' (Mark 1:8; John 1:33). The preposition is used for two or three English words, 'in, through or with'. In other words, one could also translate the phrase 'baptized in the Holy Spirit' or 'through the Holy Spirit'. The meaning remains that the believer is plunged into the Holy Spirit.

Proponents of baptism by sprinkling or pouring often use Spirit baptism to support their case. They speak of the Spirit descending on the new believer, baptizing him. The biblical picture is far more vivid, for it conveys the image of a believer being plunged into the Holy Spirit by 'Spirit baptism'.

A fifth application of our word is *death*. Jesus spoke of His coming death as a baptism (Mark 10:38). He would be overwhelmed by this death, as the baptismal candidate is overwhelmed by water in baptism. This aspect of the word is seen in secular Greek literature, where reference is made to one being 'overwhelmed by debts' (Plutarch) or an army 'overwhelming a city with misery' (Josephus).

Baptism is a comprehensive word, but its main meaning refers to the Christian initiation. When a new believer demonstrates his faith and repentance by submission to baptism, he glorifies God and completes the couplet of conversion: 'believe and be baptized' (Mark 16:16); 'repent and be baptized' (Acts 2:38).

1. G. Kirby, *Too hot to handle*, p.30.

25.
Special love

'If I speak in the tongues . . . but have not **love**' (1 Cor. 13:1)
'Love *is patient, love is kind'* (1 Cor. 13:4)
'Love *never fails'* (1 Cor. 13:8)

'Love is the queen of the graces,' wrote the Puritan Thomas Watson, 'it outshines all the others, as the sun the lesser planets.' To this sweeping statement the medieval Franciscan missionary statesman Raymond Lull (about 1232-1316) added the axiom: 'He who loves not, lives not.'

In 1 Corinthians 13 we have a hymn of love, and the focus is divine *agape* love. This is not sexual love, known to the Greeks as *eros* and forming the root of our adjective *'erotic'*. Furthermore, this is not family love, framed in the Greek word *filia* and reflected in our English term *'filial'*. Both sexual love and family love are proper in their place, but Paul here raises our sights to selfless, God-inspired love.

This brand of love is not deserved. It has its source in the heart of the lover, not in the character of the beloved. Divine love is also not limited, although human love, especially sexual love, is limited by the response of its object. (If you don't respond, I won't love you! This is pop love in the eighties.) Divine love is not selfish, seeking some advantage from the beloved. (One sees this in the philanderer who marries an obviously older and unsuitable woman, simply because of her bank balance and assets.) Divine love stands out in bold contrast to all these caricatures of Christian affection.

Agape love was featured in my previous book, *Living Words in Ephesians*.[1] However, any consideration of 1 Corinthians would be inadequate without a discussion of this scriptural masterpiece on love. Paul moves steadily and stunningly through three stages in his description of divine love.

First, he paints the background by showing the *priority of love*. Love is greater than special abilities, such as eloquence or ecstatic expression (v.1). Eloquent preaching without love is empty elocution. One recalls an evangelist who was most persuasive, but utterly unprincipled. He was an evangelical Jekyll and Hyde whose life was a lie.

Another interpretation of 'language' in verse 1 is the ecstatic tongue so loved by contemporary charismatic Christians. Without love a so-called heavenly language is nothing more than nonsense noise. It is like an alarm clock which cannot be shut off, a pain in the ear.

Love is also greater than special revelation (v.2). Balaam was a prophet without love (Num. 23-24). Caiaphas the high priest appealed to the principle of substitutionary death, but he showed no love to the Lord (John 11:50). Knowledge of the Lord was experienced by Judas Iscariot, but he responded with lies rather than love. Even apparent acts of faith can result in rejection by the Lord (Matt. 7:22).

Love is likewise greater than special sacrifices (v.3). Ananias and Sapphira made a great show of giving. They claimed to have given all they had to the Lord, but their lie masked a lack of love (Acts 5). Even martyrdom without love is nothing more than a pathetic tragedy.

Paul turns from the priority of love to the *patience of love*. Love attracts a cluster of virtues: it rejects all envy, boasting and pride (v.4). The mother of my playmate was a German. When she could no longer bear our badgering of her boy, she shrieked, '*Das ist die* limit!' Love knows no limit to its patience.

Love is likewise polite and never rude (v.5). Around the year 1600 a church history appeared. When it referred to the Lord it did so in this quaintly applicable phrase: 'It was in these days that there appeared in Judea that Knightly Gentleman Jesus Christ.' And Christ's followers are still politely 'knightly'.

Love is also positive, never given to gossip (v.6). In Bristol we have a large firm which dredges sand and gravel from the Bristol Channel. Sadly many Christians are engaged in dredging up muck and slinging it at other saints. Love never runs a dredging operation.

Love is likewise protective. It covers sin rather than exposing it to public ridicule (v.7). Love never adds up hurts and repays them in kind. It wilfully forgets slights and insults, just as the Lord did (1 Peter 2:21-22).

Finally in this great New Testament psalm Paul points to the *permanence of love*. Prophecy is partial (v.8), for it will be fulfilled.

Tongues are temporary (v.8). Some years ago a band of my students slipped into the charismatic whirlpool. After graduation they one by one came back and said, 'We have learned that ecstatic experience is too narrow a basis upon which to build a life of service.' Tongues are a sign of spiritual infancy.

Knowledge is partial (vv.8-12). It will some day be complete when we see glory firsthand. For years as a child I read about the Alps in stories like *Heidi*. Then in 1962 I saw them for the first time, and they far outshone all my reading. The best is yet to come.

Finally Paul presents his great triplet of graces: faith, hope and love (v.13 compared with Rom. 5:1-5; Col. 1:4-5; 1 Thess. 1:3). Faith will fade, when we see the Lord. Hope will hatch out into heaven. And there we shall spend all eternity loving the Lord. Faith and hope are signs of spiritual intention. These valid intentions will be realized.

It is no wonder that this chapter has attracted such accolades. Charles Hodge (1797-1878), the great American theologian, called it 'one of the jewels of Scripture'. Jamieson, Fausset and Brown in their information-filled commentary acclaim this chapter as 'the New Testament psalm of love'. Every believer finds here a standard of such exalted proportions that only God can make it work. Therefore we call it 'divine love', *agape*.

God-sized love

In 1950 the leaders of the China Inland Mission (Overseas Missionary Fellowship) were exiled from China and disorientated about the future of their missionary society. They met in Manila to assess the situation. When they could ascertain no guidance for the future, they called on Evangeline Booth (1865-1950) for advice. 'Gentlemen, how do you spell "love"?' she commenced. Their reply was impatient, 'L-o-v-e.' 'No,' the aged Salvation Army General shook her head, 'it is spelled "s-a-c-r-i-f-i-c-e".' Love in God's economy always involves sacrifice. Just as there is no cheap grace, so there is no penny-pinching love.

In Deuteronomy 6:4 *Moses* sets the tone of biblical love. 'Hear, O Israel: The Lord our God, the Lord is one.' Moses asserts elementary monotheism. Then he adds, 'Love the Lord your God with all your heart and with all your soul and with all your strength' (Deut. 6:5). Love and sacrifice are bracketed together in the eternal counsels of God. Love for the Lord liberates us from the bondage of banality and enables us to worship worthily.

In the *poetic books* we enjoy many paeans of praise to love. 'Love the Lord, all his saints!', the psalmist exhorts (Ps. 31:23). Another great love lyric is this one: 'Let those who love the Lord hate evil' (Ps. 97:10). Love to the Lord is not sentimental like a sweet sugar coating. It is rather a basic attitude of life which sacrifices recklessly for the sake of the beloved. Who is more worthy of this love than the Lord?

Crossing the border into the body of *prophetic writings*, love again asserts itself. 'I have loved you with an everlasting love,' declares our God, 'I have drawn you with loving-kindness' (Jer. 31:3). Love in God's eyes is not an accident of emotion. He is not like a teenager who falls in and out with the speed of a runaway racehorse. No, God's love is eternally reliable.

In the *Gospels* we encounter many references to love. One of the most memorable is Christ's definition of discipleship. 'As I have loved you, so you must love one another,' the Lord lays down the ground rules, 'All men will know that you are my disciples if you love one another' (John 13:34-35). One church recently sold lapel badges to its members, to identify them as committed Christians. Christ did not dictate the need of lapel badges, but rather he made love the badge of believers.

In *1 John 4* there are many references to love. According

to John's command, 'Dear friends, let us love one another, for love comes from God. Everyone who loves has been born of God and knows God' (1 John 4:7). 'God is love,' and love belongs to the very essence of deity (1 John 4:16). In fact, Augustine found the eternal love of God to be implicit proof of the Trinity. Since God eternally loved, he must have had an eternal object of his love. This argues for more than one person in the Godhead.

Love is so large that a smaller chapter is almost an insult to the theme. According to tradition, the apostle John gave a good example of his pet theme, when he was very old. When he could no longer walk, he was carried by Christians into the assembly. Lifting himself up on one elbow the apostle would say, 'Brothers, "love one another." This is the Lord's command.'

1. Pages 65-68.

26.
Speak in tongues

'Anyone who **speaks in tongues***'* (1 Cor. 14:2)
'He who **speaks in a tongue** *edifies himself'* (1 Cor. 14:4)
'If I **pray in a tongue***'* (1 Cor. 14:14)

Had I written this chapter twenty years ago, it would have levitated in the realms of theory. Since the mid-sixties, however, tongues have become a lightning flash throughout the church. Theoretical teaching is as out-of-date as an abacus in the age of computers.

In 1964 the South African pioneer of neo-pentecostalism, David DuPlessis spearheaded the charismatic movement among Anglicans, and he even addressed the General Assembly of the Church of Scotland. The next year Dennis Bennett, the renewal rector of St Luke's in Seattle, extended his experience to both church and academic circles in the United Kingdom.

One of the primary proponents of charismatic renewal among Anglicans is David Watson, the former vicar of St Michael-le-Belfrey in York. 'More and more churches, ministers, missionaries, Christians of varying degrees of maturity, are testifying to some charismatic experience,' Watson wrote.[1]

Don Basham was a pastor in Canada and the United States, but now he is an apologist for the charismatic movement. 'The church is in the midst of world-wide revival and . . . central to that revival is the experience we call the baptism in the Holy Spirit,' Basham asserts. Then he adds, 'Central to the baptism in the Holy Spirit is a phenomenon called "Glossolalia" or speaking in tongues.'[2]

The word used by Basham was 'glossolalia', and it is the Greek word we shall now consider. Actually, it is two Greek words: *glosso* ('tongue')[3] and *lalein* ('to speak'). Combined, these two words become a technical term for the phenomenon which Paul ponders in 1 Corinthians 12-14. It is in chapter 14 that he really comes to grips with the thorny issue. There are six reasons why Paul plays down tongues.

First, tongues are primarily for private benefit. 'Anyone who speaks in a tongue, does not speak to men but to God,' Paul presupposes (1 Cor. 14:2). The result is self-edifying (1 Cor. 14:4) and unintelligible prayer (1 Cor. 14:14). Tongues, even in Pauline times, were mainly a matter of personal piety, and thus they did not enhance the church.

Second, tongues are less preferable than preaching. 'Prophecy' in 1 Corinthians 14 includes the elements of biblical preaching: 'strengthening, encouragement, comfort' (1 Cor. 14:3) derived from 'revelation, knowledge, prophecy, instruction' (1 Cor. 14:6). Tongues captivate the emotions, but biblical preaching captures the mind for God.

Third, tongues preclude profitable prayer. If someone prays in tongues, how can another person identify with that prayer and say the 'Amen'? (1 Cor. 14:13-16.) Prayer is not only a private affair, but it is also a corporate experience. This corporate aspect of prayer is lost when the person praying lapses into tongues.

Fourth, Paul saw glossolalia as second-class charisma. 'I speak in tongues more than all of you,' Paul admitted (1 Cor. 14:18). Most of my charismatic friends stop there, but Paul goes on, 'In the church I would rather speak five intelligible words to instruct others than ten thousand words in a tongue' (1 Cor. 14:19). Paul found tongues to be of virtually no value to the assembled church.

Fifth, tongues confuse the non-Christian. Although tongues should be a sign to unbelievers (1 Cor. 14:22), they thoroughly confuse the visitor to worship (1 Cor. 14:23). Every pastor has probably had the experience. A new Christian or non-Christian is exposed to ecstatic utterance and is totally confused. Now, the object is not to overcome their antipathy towards tongues, but to lead them to the Lord.

Sixth, tongues imperil the order in worship. According to Paul, 'God is not a God of disorder but of peace' (1 Cor. 14:33). 'Everything should be done in a fitting and orderly way' (1 Cor. 14:40). There is much talk about liberty in the Spirit, but often this devolves into licence without the Spirit.

Tongues in perspective

When Tom Flynn burst into print to describe the Catholic charismatic movement in Ireland, he insisted, 'Tongues is the gift that is most commonly received after the baptism in the Holy Spirit.'[4]

Transatlantic soul mates of Flynn are Kevin and Dorothy Ranaghan. In their book on the Catholic experience, they recount a charismatic prayer meeting in South Bend, Indiana, home of Notre Dame University, the foremost Catholic university. One unlearned man prayed the 'Hail Mary' in Greek, a language he had never learned. According to the Ranaghans, the prayer meetings took on a decidedly Marian flavour. (Incidentally, in some research I did into the Catholic renewal movement, I discovered a deepened devotion to the mass, Mary and the sacraments.)

We must, however, return to consider some complementary passages to 1 Corinthians 14. In Mark 16:17 there is the first reference to 'new tongues' as one of the signs identifying believers.

The first principle concerning tongues is this: *they are not a singular gift*. They are accompanied by other equal gifts, such as exorcism, protection from poisonous snakes and drinks, and instantaneous healing (Mark 16:17-18). In Paul's perception, tongues are actually way down on the totem-pole of spiritual gifts (1 Cor. 12:7-10, 27-30). Why is it that modern-day proponents of tongues have turned this Pauline order on its head? Perhaps it arises from a singular lack of the more helpful and less spectacular gifts.

A second principle is this: *tongues in the early church soon faded*. At Pentecost the early Christians spoke in tongues and communicated the message of Messiah (Acts 2:4, 11). However, subsequent references to the Jerusalem church reveal no further emphasis on tongues. Could it be that they were no longer in use?

At the outset of the Ephesian church tongues confirmed the coming of the Holy Spirit (Acts 19:6). However, neither Paul's Ephesian letter, nor the instructions to Timothy, nor the letter to Ephesus in Revelation 2:1-7 make any further reference to tongues. Now the argument from silence is always weak, but such a deafening silence might just indicate that tongues had ceased at Ephesus, too.

A third principle is this: *tongues in the early church were not of primary importance.* According to Paul, tongues were eclipsed by love (1 Cor. 13:8) and prophecy (1 Cor. 14:1-5). When tongues are extinguished, love will still be burning brightly (1 Cor. 13:8). This throws cold water over the assertion of Derek Prince that a Spirit-baptized believer without tongues is like an elephant without a trunk. I say, on the basis of 1 Corinthians 12-14, that this assertion violates the New Testament in spirit and statement.

Speaking in tongues is an indication of spiritual infancy. Paul puts forward this principle in 1 Corinthians 12, and experience bears it out. Those who speak in tongues may very well be sincere Christians, but as they grow they will gain a hunger for more of God. This can only be satisfied by the Scriptures. To paraphrase Hebrews 5:12-6:3, let us go on from the spiritual 'junk food' of ecstatic experience to the staple diet of scriptural truth.

1. D. Watson, *One in the Spirit*, p.65.
2. Don W. Basham, *Ministering the Baptism in the Holy Spirit*, p.28.
3. See W. Detzler, *Living Words in 1 Peter*, pp.68-71.
4. T. Flynn, *The Charismatic Renewal and the Irish Experience*, p.79.

27.
Order, order

'Everything should be done in a fitting and **orderly** *way'*
(1 Cor. 14:40)

When Ramon Hunston wrote his popular biography of George Thomas, he titled the slim volume, *Order, Order*. When broadcasting from the House of Commons was introduced, the British public became accustomed to the Welsh accent of George Thomas, the Christian gentleman and Speaker of the House. The white-hot verbal pyrotechnics of the Commons cooled down only reluctantly to the cry of Mr Thomas, 'Order, order'.

It is the word 'order' that we now take for consideration. In the Greek form it is *taxis* and it reflects such meanings as 'fixed succession, orderly manner, position or post, and even the appearance of order'. English actually abounds with hints of our word, *taxis*. Some English indications are '*taxi*dermy' which arranges animals for show by stuffing them, obviously after their demise. Another example is '*tax*onomy' which is the science of classification or order. (Lest our minds run riot let's remember that 'tax' in the financial sense arises from the Latin *taxare*, 'to touch, censure or value'.)

For the purposes of this consideration, we look at two appearances of the word *taxis* in 1 Corinthians. The first is found in a section dealing with worship. In the ministry 'everything should be done in a fitting and orderly way' (1 Cor. 14:40). Placed as it is at the end of 1 Corinthians 14, this really summarizes most of the letter. Paul has dealt with disorder in the church. In doing so he has detected disorder (1 Cor. 14:33) in cliques among Christians (chs 1-3), immorality in the church (ch.5), lawsuits between believers (ch.6), emasculation of marriage (ch.7), flirtation with idolatry (ch.8), gluttony at the Lord's Table (chs 10-11), and a free-for-all in worship (chs 12-14). It is no wonder that he concludes this section by crying, 'Order, order'!

The Corinthian church looked like a teenaged boy's bedroom. Everything was out of place, with clothes hung from the chair. Remnants of beauty were broken on the floor, like discarded toys. There was even ample evidence of dust under the bed. The church was as chaotic as a child's room, and Paul set about to clean it up.

A further appearance of our word is found in 1 Corinthians. Here the emphasis falls on a more positive note. The first converts in Greece came from the house of one Stephanas, Stephen. Their distinguishing characteristic was this: 'they have devoted' (*tasso*, 'ordered') 'themselves to the service of the saints' (1 Cor. 16:15).

What a dramatic contrast the Stephanas family offered to the prevailing pandemonium at Corinth! Little else is known about them other than their baptism at Paul's hand (1 Cor. 1:16). However, their devotion to service is marked for our instruction and imitation nearly two millennia later.

This Pauline pattern of order is not implicit in the natural order of things. In fact, nature in its raw state shows a remarkable lack of order. Recently I tried to tame a certain corner of our garden, after the briar bushes attacked me, cutting my finger. As I chatted over the garden fence with my neighbour, I lamented the lack of order in that corner. 'Weeds always grow best,' my wise and friendly neighbour claimed, 'they will always do better than the blossoms.'

My friend did not refer directly to the Eden affair, but he certainly stated a biblical principle. God set man in a perfect environment. Then man disobeyed God's order of things, and ever since chaos has competed with order. Apart from the redemptive gardening of God, chaos conquers order.

Apple pie order

Many Bible truths are beyond the reach of reason. Creation is shrouded in the wordless mists of cosmic history, and it is only revealed through the divine record of Genesis. The selection process whereby God chose Israel is also a mystery to us.

Christ's conception outside the process of human procreation is also beyond our ability to apprehend.

On the other hand, God's order of things is an ambassador from eternity. He created order in the universe to give us a clue to the Creator. In his historical dealings with man there is likewise order to indicate his sovereignty. Most obviously, in redemption there is a discernible order or plan, which points to his providence. Order is thus a handle on eternity, allowing limited man to get a grip on the infinite God.

Our word *taxis* meant many things to the New Testament writer. First, it described a particular *group of people*. 'Zechariah's division' ('order') 'was on duty and he was serving as priest before God' (Luke 1:8). Today we see this idea echoed in Roman Catholic orders, such as the Order of St Francis or the Order of St Augustine. In other circles ministers are 'ordained', or 'take holy orders'.

A second New Testament use of our word is a *position or post*. The mysterious (presumed second-century) Epistle to Diognetus acclaimed eminent Christians and rejoiced that 'God has appointed them to so great a position'. The same idea is reflected in Romans 13:1, where Paul urges obedience to authorities who are 'established' (*hypertasso*, ordered) 'by God'.

This divine ordering of human affairs gives us confidence, even when we cannot see because of the smoke of human conflict. Recently Sir Winston Churchill's underground war centre in Whitehall was opened to public view. There the great statesman directed the far-flung operations of his forces and liaised with leaders in the Allied capitals. Who would doubt that God gave us Churchill for the war years to help purge the plague of a hysterical Hitler from the scene?

The third meaning of our word is an *orderly manner*. The apostle Paul commended Colossian Christians for their 'orderly' life and firm faith (Col. 2:5). Spiritual life and ordered life are not opposed to each other. They are two sides of the same coin. When the Holy Spirit reigns supreme in life, he creates an order which defies description.

The Quaker hymn-writer and social activist John Greenleaf Whittier (1807-92) expressed biblical truth when he wrote,

Take from our souls the strain and stress,
And let our ordered lives confess
The beauty of Thy peace.

A final purpose of our term is *appearance or quality*. Seven
out of ten uses of our word *taxis* in the New Testament are
found in Hebrews. They refer to the king-priest Melchizedek.
The Lord is 'a priest for ever in the *order* of Melchizedek'
(Heb. 5:6). This same formulation is found in Hebrews 5:10;
6:20 and 7:11. Obviously order here does not refer to a class
of individuals, since only two priests of Melchizedek are ever
mentioned: the patriarchal King of Jerusalem and the
messianic King of Peace, the Lord Jesus Christ. This forces
Greek students to infer that order also contains the idea of
appearance or quality.

God's order of things operates on a vastly different plane
from ours. God produces priests who are eternal, but our
ordination dies when 'Reverend' is chiselled on our gravestone.
God embues his order of priests with glory that is heavenly
in its hue; our human glory is often tarnished by imperfection.
Order in God's view is moral and thus achieves our best,
whereas human order is too often geared to expedience.

Therefore we allow the Holy Spirit to place his order on
our worship. Only then can we worship in a fitting and orderly
way.

28.
Resurrection hope

'No **resurrection** *of the dead'* (1 Cor. 15: 12-13)
'The **resurrection** *of the dead comes through man'* (1 Cor. 15:21)

Resurrection is a fact of life. One cannot restrict the subject to Easter, for it is an underlying theme of all Christian revelation and declaration. Neither can the resurrection be limited to the Lord Jesus Christ, for he has demonstrated a revivifying reality which will embrace all people.

Writers from many quarters have referred to the resurrection as fact. Horace Bushnell (1802-76), the Congregational theologian, declared, 'The resurrection of Jesus Christ is absolutely the best attested fact in ancient history.' The law professor Sir Norman Anderson viewed the resurrection from the standpoint of a barrister. 'There is no point in arguing about the empty tomb,' insisted Sir Norman. 'Everyone, friend or opponent, knew that it was empty. The only questions worth arguing about were why it was empty and what the emptiness proved.' At the end of the first century, (about 93/94), the Jew Josephus wrote, 'He [Jesus] appeared to them alive on the third day.'

This sense of assurance permeates every page of New Testament revelation. The word 'resurrection' is a translation of the Greek term *anastasis* (from the verb *anistēmi*, 'to stand up'). One sees the word transliterated in such a name as 'Anastasia'. The noun occurs thirty-nine times in the New Testament, while the verb appears thirty-eight times.

In 1 Corinthians 15:12-13 the emphasis falls on a general truth. All human beings will be resurrected from the dead. Although some will be raised to judgement, those who are related by repentance and faith to Christ will be resurrected to eternal life and bliss. The guarantee of general resurrection is the resurrection of Christ. Although Christ resuscitated three people (Jairus's daughter, the young man at Nain and Lazarus), they all died again. The only real resurrection was that of Jesus, who rose never to die again.

The Christian message stands or falls with the resurrection of Christ. According to the noted seventeenth-century Bible commentator John Trapp (1601-69), 'Never was there as great an imposture put upon the world as Christianity, if Christ be yet in the grave.'

The apostle Paul refers to an oft-repeated contrast between Adam and Christ: 'For since death came through a man [Adam], the resurrection of the dead comes also through a man [Christ]' (1 Cor. 15:21). The resurrection of Christ has consequences for our salvation. It reveals that God accepts Christ's sacrifice on our behalf. According to Studdert Kennedy, a lesser-known writer, 'If Christ be not risen, the dreadful consequence is not that death ends life, but that we are still in our sins.'

In this practical exposition of resurrection, the apostle describes what will happen. 'So will it be with the resurrection of the dead. The body that is sown is perishable, it is raised imperishable' (1 Cor. 15:42). Although we cannot imagine the post-resurrection body, we do know that our glorified body will never suffer, become senile or indeed succumb to death.

The Gospels do not explain the resurrection; the resurrection explains the Gospels,' concluded John S. Whale. 'Belief in the resurrection is not an appendage to the Christian faith; it is the Christian faith.'

There is no ambiguity in the biblical presentation of resurrection. Christ was raised from the dead, and this is as authentic as his death. If reporters seeking hard news had gone to the grave on the first Easter morning, they would have found an empty tomb, which could have been photographed, had today's technology been available.

Resurrection-hope or hazard?

A packed audience gathered to hear a Russian lecturer speak

about the resurrection of Christ. With withering sarcasm the speaker scorned the very idea that Jesus could have been raised from the dead. At length the Marxist orator finished. At the back of the hall an old man in the garb of an Orthodox priest stood to his feet to ask a question.

'Sir,' queried the old gentleman, 'may I have a few moments to refute your presentation?'

'Five minutes,' snapped the speaker, 'you can have five minutes.'

'I shall only require five seconds,' replied the priest as he made his way to the front. Then he shouted the traditional eastern Easter greeting: 'Christ is risen!'

'He is risen indeed,' the crowd answered with a thunderous roar.

Turning to the perplexed lecturer, the priest submitted, 'Sir, I rest my case.'

There are two basic settings for our word *anastasis* in the New Testament. The first is predictable: the *resurrection of Christ*. When the apostle Paul preached before a philosophically sophisticated audience at Athens, he preached 'the good news about Jesus and the resurrection' (Acts 17:18). The Athenians assumed that Paul was preaching about two gods: 'Jesus and the resurrection' (Acts 17:18). However, Paul persisted in proclaiming the resurrection of the Lord (Acts 17:31-32).

The resurrection is not only the high note of apostolic preaching, it is also the cornerstone of Christian hope. Christians are 'united with him in his resurrection' (Rom. 6:5). Their practice of baptism by immersion presented a continuing demonstration of resurrection truth (Rom. 6:4).

Christians also believed that the resurrection of Christ infused them with a new power. They spoke of experiencing 'the power of his resurrection' (Phil. 3:10). The fact of the resurrection fired feeble Christians with hope and courage. It was this resurrection which demonstrated God's dynamic for saving sinners (1 Peter 3:21). 'He was delivered over to death for our sins and was raised to life for our justification' (Rom. 4:25).

Although he would not be counted as an evangelical in our

mould, William Hordern asserted the resurrection eloquently in his *Layman's Guide to Protestant Theology*: 'The Resurrection proclaims the fact that there is a power at work in the world which is mightier than all the forces that crucified our Lord. The resurrection is not just a personal survival of the man Jesus . . . it is a cosmic victory.'[1]

The second application of our word *anastasis* is the companion truth of the *general resurrection*. It is here that we see the hazard of the resurrection. 'A time is coming when all who are in their graves will hear his [the Son of Man's] voice,' warned Jesus, 'those who have done good will rise to live, and those who have done evil will rise to be condemned' (John 5:28-29). The truth of judgement is here implanted in the context of resurrection.

It was Paul's commitment to the coming resurrection which brought him into conflict with Jewish authorities. The Pharisees, of whom Paul was one, believed in the resurrection. However, the Sadducees sneered at the resurrection (Acts 23:8). There is, of course, a similar tension between people in our time. Many modern secular scientists sweep away any thought of the resurrection. However, one recalls Werner von Braun, the noted German scientist, who argued cogently from the continuance of matter that life must exist after death. The only change would be a change in form.

Whenever the apostles wrote about essential faith, they included teaching about the resurrection. In fact, the writer of Hebrews listed basic beliefs of Christians: 'baptisms, the laying on of hands, the resurrection of the dead, and eternal judgement' (Heb. 6:2).

No more effective argument for the reality of resurrection exists than that of Richard Baxter, the great Puritan preacher and author. A workman can turn basic elements into glass, and a seed springs forth into flowers. Similarly an acorn gives rise to an oak. 'Why should we doubt whether the seed of everlasting life and glory, which is now in the blessed souls with Christ,' reasons Baxter, 'can by him communicate a perfection to the flesh that is dissolved into its elements?'

1. W. Horden, *Layman's Guide to Protestant Theology*, New York: The MacMillan Co., 1955, p.205.

29.
Dress up

'The perishable must **clothe itself** *with the imperishable'*
(1 Cor. 15:53)

'Clothes make the man,' most mothers tell their sons when they send them out into the world of work. Within a few years a wife takes up the same refrain, and this keeps the men's outfitters in business.

Some years ago while serving as pastor of a small church I splurged and bought a suit. It was paid for with birthday money from my parents in America. The next Sunday I overheard one young woman in the church ask another: 'Have you seen the pastor in his birthday suit?' Needless to say, that question was revised before it was repeated!

The subject of suits also has a metaphorical meaning. It was projected into full form by the gifted word-smith and prime minister, Benjamin Disraeli (1804-91). In a parliamentary debate on 28 February 1845 he spoke of Sir Robert Peel. 'The Right Hon. Gentleman [Peel] caught the Whigs bathing,' Disraeli declared, 'and walked away with their clothes.'

The word under consideration is *enduo* (to 'clothe', or to 'put on'). It is transliterated into English and found in our word 'endue'. The meaning is broad but well defined. It means to invest or impute some honour, like the Investiture of the Prince of Wales in Caernarvon Castle. A second meaning of 'endue' is to endow or provide financially for someone, like the endowments which establish certain professorial chairs in universities. A final meaning is to clothe with grace or favour, and a beautiful woman may be said to be endued with loveliness.

In 1 Corinthians, however, *enduo* is used in a unique sense. When a Christian dies the real person, the immaterial man or woman, speeds to heaven. Later on when the Lord returns and resurrects the saints, the person will be 'clothed' with a brand-new body, an 'eternal birthday suit'. The 'perishable must clothe itself with the imperishable' (1 Cor. 15:53-54).

To die is to be divested of a worn-out garment. Just as we throw away a tattered sweater with frayed edges and holes in the elbows, we also part with the body at death. Now, that old sweater is worn out simply *because* we have enjoyed wearing it so long. In the same way we are very attached to our bodies. We recognize our friends partially by appearance. However, at death we gladly give up the broken-down body knowing that a better version will soon be provided, and it will never wear out.

The same picture is also found in Paul's second letter to the Corinthians. After describing in detail the decadence of the body, Paul exults, 'When we are clothed, we will not be found naked . . . [we shall be] clothed with our heavenly dwelling' (2 Cor. 5:2-3). When we move into our permanent and palatial home in heaven, we shall have a new wardrobe to match, a 'glory gown'.

The ancients used to debate about the number of angels who could polka on a pin-head. In olden times they also discussed the business of after-death dress. Paul's young contemporary, Rabbi Eliezer, put the minds of Jews at rest when he discussed the nature of resurrection robes. According to Eliezer, there would be no nakedness at the resurrection. He assured his followers that the resurrected would be clothed in shrouds. Is this the reason we often lay out corpses in their best suits?[1]

Laying trivia to one side, we rejoice in the news that we shall have a new resurrection body. The most robust of us will be glad to be free from the head-colds, toothache and assorted disadvantages of our current bodies. It is the Lord who has already modelled our resurrected body, and he will provide one for us when he returns.

Sunday-go-to-meeting

In the industrial, working-class community where I grew up, most people had one good suit of clothes. Every Sunday it showed up when they went to worship. This gave rise to the amazing adjective clause: 'Sunday-go-to-meeting'. Sundays they wore their 'Sunday-go-to-meeting' clothes, their 'Sunday best'. In fact, a homely gospel song expressed a profound aspiration. 'I want to be more,' prayed the poet, 'than a "Sunday-go-to-meeting" Christian.'

Actually the Greek word *enduo* has only two elementary strings to its bow. First, it is used for *putting on clothes*. Jesus used it when he urged his followers: 'Do not worry about your life, what you will eat or drink; or about your body, what you will wear' (put on) (Matt. 6:25). Nature nurtures their faith, when they see that 'God clothes the grass of the field' (Matt. 6:30). (The word used to describe God's clothing of the flowers is *amphiennumi*, a less common verb.)

The point is this: God cares for our clothing and sees that we have sufficient. Deprived of normal clothing, the slaves of America's southern states looked forward to heaven. One of their spirituals spotlighted God's provision:

> I got shoes, you got shoes, all God's children got shoes,
> When I get to heaven, gonna put on my shoes,
>   gonna walk all over God's heaven.
> I got a robe, you got a robe, all God's children got a robe,
> When I get to heaven, gonna put on my robe,
>   gonna walk all over God's heaven.

A current example is an academic procession, where each graduate is properly clothed. I recall that hot July day in Manchester when I donned a scarlet robe with gold trimming. Then I draped around my neck a golden hood, and topped it all off with a grandly distinctive head-dress. Less than an hour later I took it off after receiving my doctoral diploma. When I get to heaven I'll have a robe of righteousness that will never have to be taken back. God will provide it: it will not come from some academic rental agency.

The second aspect of our word *enduo* speaks of *putting on character*. To the Romans Paul wrote, 'Clothe yourselves with the Lord Jesus, and do not think about how to gratify the desires of the sinful nature' (Rom. 13:14).

The Christian clothes himself in the character of Christ. Consequently he resembles the Redeemer more each day. Charles Sheldon (1857-1946), an American Congregationalist clergyman, wrote *In His Steps* (1896). It dramatized the idea that Christians should strive to do in every situation what Jesus would have done. The principle is Pauline: 'Clothe yourselves with the Lord Jesus.'

In other places Paul urges Christians to 'put on the new self, created to be like God in true righteousness and holiness' (Eph. 4:24, compared with Col. 3:10). Clothes make such a difference. Think of the many remnants of the 'hippy age' who are now in our churches: they are saved, shaved, showered, suited and serving the Lord.

Yet another application of this spiritual 'suitability' is seen in Paul's preference for spiritual armour against Satan's strokes (Eph. 6:11; Rom. 13:12; 1 Thess. 5:8). Taking a pattern from Roman guards, Paul promises protection to all who wear the armour of the Lord.

Christians are like ice hockey goalkeepers. Their face is protected by a mask, and almost every inch of their body is padded. Their feet have especially strengthened skates and their hands padded mittens. Similarly, the Christian is completely clothed against the missiles that Satan lets fly.

If we worried less about what we wear on the outside and more about our spiritual suits, we would be more suitable for serving the Lord.

1. James Moffat, *The First Epistle to the Corinthians*, p.258.

30.
How to save

'Set aside a sum of money . . . **saving** *it up'* (1 Cor. 16:2)

When he was pressed for his views on money, John Wesley put it this way: 'Make all you can, save all you can, give all you can.' Now saving is big business. The proliferation of banks and building societies demonstrates this.

Many businessmen have combined Christian commitment with commercial acumen. In England none has been more well known than Sir John Laing (1879-1978). When he died at age ninety-eight the obituaries were hymns of praise. It was, however, the statement of his estate that most impressed me. 'Sir John Laing, the building industry pioneer . . . was president of the multi-million pound Laing group of companies before his death in January, aged 98,' the *Sunday Telegraph* reported the facts. Then the journalist added that Sir John left only £371 net. The explanation was magnificent: 'The small net sum reflects Sir John's lifelong dedication to Christian and philanthropic work.'

There is no doubt about it, Sir John Laing knew how to make money. But he also knew how to save it. He saved it because he gave it away. This has left him not only with an immense reserve of goodwill on earth, but also with treasures in his heavenly retirement home.

Our word in 1 Corinthians is the Greek verb *thesaurizein* (to store up, gather or save). Usually it is employed to explain the hoarding of material possessions or money. In English it is seen in a latinized form, 'thesaurus'. This describes a collection of words, and it arises from the Latin word for treasury or storehouse, *thesaurus*.

Paul appropriated our word in teaching Corinthians about the concept of charitable giving. Famine had swept the Palestine population leaving Christians in Jerusalem in deep distress. So the apostles gathered relief funds and took them to the Jerusalem church. Paul impressed upon individual Christians that each should 'set aside a sum of money in keeping with his income, saving it up' *(thesauron)*' (1 Cor. 16:2).

In fact, the apostle asserts four principles of Christian giving which still hold valid. First, it is to be planned: 'On the first day of every week, each one of you should set aside a sum of money' (1 Cor. 16:2). Second, it is personal: 'each one' gives. Third, the gift is to be proportionate: 'in keeping with his income'. And finally, it is to be practical — for the distressed Christians in Jerusalem.

Christian giving is not a secondary and somewhat embarrassed passing of a gratuity to God, as one slips a coin into the hand of a hat-check girl at a posh restaurant. No, Christian giving is rooted in worship and expresses the proper reaction of Christian thankfulness.

A further feature of our word is found in 2 Corinthians. The gospel is here described as a 'treasure' *(thesauros)* 'in jars of clay' (2 Cor. 4:7). The message of man's redemption is deposited in the hearts, minds and mouths of fallible folk. It is an eternal treasure in a temporal treasury. In fact, the humanness of Christian workers is so obvious that a friend of mine threatened to write a book entitled *Feet of Clay*. Had he been a more persistent penman, the book would have exposed the foibles of fellow Christians. All his friends are thankful for his literary lethargy that saves their reputations.

The final outcropping of the term *thesaurizein* is in the cryptic comment of Paul: 'Children should not have to save up' *(thesaurizein)* 'for their parents, but parents for their children' (2 Cor. 12:14). Here the apostle was urging the Corinthian Christians to receive their spiritual parent, and in so doing he enunciated an undisputed principle. Parents pass on a legacy to their children, and they do not expect children to support them.

In this brief survey of the Corinthian correspondence, we have seen that our word is used both in terms of material and also spiritual stores. We store up money to be used for God's glory, but we also have received a store of spiritual treasures to be passed on.

Treasury without debt

Now the word 'treasure' or 'treasury' conjures up in our mind central government. The national treasury seems to have as its aim the snatching away of our personal treasury by means of tax.

Wernher von Braun (1912-1977), the German rocket expert, consoled the long-suffering and large-spending American tax-payer. 'There is just one thing I can promise you about the outer-space program,' von Braun conceded, 'your tax dollar will go farther.'

Von Braun's impish boast was rather closely connected to an earlier statement by Herbert Hoover (1874-1964). 'Blessed are the young,' comforted the much-maligned president, 'for they shall inherit the national debt.'

Most human treasuries are saddled with debt. Over-spending soars out of sight, and the indebtedness is expressed in millions and billions. Meanwhile most normal people agonize about an overdraft of tens or hundreds. In God's treasury there is no overdraft, however. He can cover any expenditure.

The repository of all God's riches is in *Christ*. To the Colossians Paul wrote of Christ: 'in whom are hidden all the treasures' *(thesauroi)* 'of wisdom and knowledge' (Col. 2:3). Our need will never be large enough to exhaust that deposit. In fact, all the need of all the believers who have lived or ever will live will not diminish the deposit at all.

It is like the royal family. When a prince is born his future is assured. As he grows up he lives under an artificial limitation. When he reaches maturity he is given his share of the phenomenal wealth of the family. The difference between a British prince and a heavenly prince is this: God's children get the full treasury of Christ at birth, or rather rebirth.

The heavenly treasure releases us from dependence on *earthly treasure*. Moses counted the endurance of 'disgrace for the sake of Christ as of greater value than the treasures' *(thesauroi)* 'of Egypt' (Heb. 11:26).

We see this comparison in everyday life. Wealthy people are cocooned in luxury, but this all becomes valueless when trouble hits. No amount of money can buy back broken health, or restore cracked confidence, or mend a marriage gone wrong. The real treasures are not totted up on a calculator.

A third use of treasure is our *treasure in heaven*. Christ exhorted his followers to 'store up for yourselves treasures in heaven' (Matt. 6:19-20). These are safe from rust, rot, ruin and robbery.

One thinks of a Sunday School teacher whose work has led to the conversion of a lad, like Edward Kimball who taught Dwight L. Moody the doctrines of grace and saw Moody converted. Years later Kimball's son was converted in a meeting where Moody preached.[1] What a treasure Edward Kimball collected!

The fourth aspect of treasure is negative: this is the *storehouse of wrath*. To the unrepentant Paul says, 'You are storing up wrath against yourself for the day of God's wrath' (Rom. 2:5). A world in rebellion against God is 'reserved for fire, being kept [treasured] for the day of judgement and destruction of ungodly men' (2 Peter 3:7).

Just as Christians accumulate treasure in glory, so unbelievers are storing up suffering in hell. After death the treasury is unlocked and God declares an eternal dividend.

It makes sense therefore to follow the command of Christ. 'Sell your possessions and give to the poor,' Jesus advised, 'and you will have treasure in heaven' (Matt. 19:21). The hymn-writer Anna L. Waring (1820-1910) had it right when she wrote,

> My hope I cannot measure,
> My path to life is free;
> My Saviour has my treasure,
> And He will walk with me.

1. W.R. Moody, *The Life of Dwight L. Moody*, p.40.

31.
Open door

*'A great **door** for effective work has opened to me'* (1 Cor. 16:9)

In many ways, doors are the face of a house or any other building. They are either inviting or infuriating. When we first came to Kensington Baptist Church in Bristol the church doors were a sickening shade of purple. Our church was famous, or rather infamous, for those disgusting doors. Brides schemed to have their wedding photos taken anywhere but in front of our faded doors. Finally a courageous caretaker took matters into his own hands and brushed the horrible hue out of existence. Most of us were instantly thankful, but some hankered for the 'good old doors'.

Doors declare a welcome or a warning. Not far from our manse is one of Her Majesty's hotels, a high-security prison. Whenever my ministry takes me inside, I must first gain entrance through the massive wooden doors. A prison officer opens a small door in the large gates and lets me in. Despite the friendly humour of the officer, I feel decidedly uneasy when I walk through the door and the lock slams shut behind me.

The Greek word for door is *thura* and it is used thirty-eight times in the New Testament. It is most perfectly reflected in the German word for door, *Tür*.

When Paul used the word 'door' he often meant it metaphorically. We have a similar idea in the phrase, 'opportunity knocks'. When the chance to improve ourselves comes, we hasten to heed the call. In this same vein Paul wrote to the Corinthians, 'I will stay on at Ephesus until Pentecost, because a great door for effective work has opened to me' (1 Cor. 16:8-9). The apostle was awake to any open door to declare the gospel. When opportunity arose he did not hang about, but rather rushed in and stayed until he was figuratively or even physically thrown out.

The Pauline penchant for capitalizing on chances to serve

the Lord was summarized by Miguel des Cervantes (1547-1616), the creator of *Don Quixote*. 'When one door is shut,' he concluded, 'another opens.' The apostolic hopscotch around the Mediterranean certainly served to substantiate Cervantes' axiom. It must be noted, however, that Paul knew that *God* opened doors. This is not a shot in the dark or a game of cosmic Russian roulette.

In 2 Corinthians Paul again returns to the picture of an open door. When he landed in Troas he 'found that the Lord had opened a door' (2 Cor. 2:12). So Paul pursued it and preached until day dawned, only pausing to resuscitate poor old Eutychus (Acts 20:7-12).

Somehow I think Paul could have understood the thinking of Ralph Waldo Emerson (1803-1882), a Unitarian forefather of my wife: 'If a man write a better book, preach a better sermon, or make a better mousetrap than his neighbour,' theorized the poetic philosopher, 'though he build his house in the woods, the world will make a beaten path to his door.'

Paul did not care much where the door of opportunity was hung. Wherever he saw God had swung it open, he went in and preached. That is why Europe got the gospel, and Asia got Islam. God opened the door to Greece and closed the door to Asia Minor.

In or out

For several months I noticed a particularly striking parish church near Bristol docks. When my friend became vicar we attended the service of institution. Only when I strolled smugly up to the magnificent portico did I realize that the entrance was elsewhere. We duly detoured to the side door where we were able to enter. The lesson is simple: apparently open doors are sometimes more apparent than open.

Many Bible stories have doors prominently placed. Our word is used for the *door of buildings*. When the apostolic age dawned, the apostles were crouched inside 'with the doors locked for fear of the Jews' (John 20:19). The Lord ignored the security system. 'Though the doors were locked,'

John remembered under the Holy Spirit's stimulus, 'Jesus came and stood among them' (John 20:26). Obviously, the resurrected Lord did not worry greatly about locked doors.

In his hymn, 'Let all the world in ev'ry corner sing,' George Herbert (1593-1633), the Elizabethan Rector of Bemerton, caught the concept of passing through doors:

> The church with psalms must shout,
> No door can shut them out:
> But above all the heart
> Must bear the longest part.

Another use of door is *opportunity*. When returning from their first missionary journey, Paul and Barnabas brought a report to the church at Antioch. 'They gathered the church together and reported all that God had done through them and how he had opened the door of faith to the Gentiles' (Acts 14:27). At the end of his life Paul was imprisoned at Rome. To him prison was not a closed door but an opening. 'Pray for us,' Paul petitioned the Colossians, 'that God may open a door for our message' (Col. 4:3).

Such an open door is demonstrated in the life of Dwight L. Moody (1837-1899), who moved west to Chicago at age nineteen in 1856. Two years later he had discovered a remarkable realm of service and founded a Sunday School with upwards of 600 children. The remainder of his life was a series of similarly open doors in America and Britain.

A third door is the *entrance to heaven*. On the Mount of Olives Jesus explained to his men: 'When you see all these things, you know that it [the end time] is near, right at the door' (Matt. 24:33). Those who hesitate to prepare, however, will find themselves standing before a closed door (Matt. 25:10).

Unbelievers see death as a door, but it is only a way out into the abyss. The English dramatist John Webster (1580?-1625?) portrayed this dismal impression in his *The Duchess of Malfi*: 'I know death hath ten thousand several doors, for men to take their exits.'

There is, of course, one final door. *The Lord* is the Door.

According to his own words, 'I am the gate' (door); 'whoever enters through me will be saved. He will come in and go out and find pasture' (John 10:9). The same statement is repeated in John 10:1, 2, 7.

Human doors may or may not provide hope and help. In fact, Edward Fitzgerald (1809-1883) laments this lack in his famous *Rubaiyat of Omar Khayyam*:

> Myself when young did eagerly frequent
> Doctor and Saint and heard great argument
> About it and about: but evermore
> Came out by the same Door as in I went.

What an everlasting relief it is to know that entering into Christ as the Door is more satisfying! Lawyers, doctors and counsellors can only give good advice, but Christ alone is the Door to life more abundant.

32.
Work overtime

'*Carry on the* **work** *of the Lord*' (1 Cor. 16:10)
'*Everyone who joins in the* **work**' (1 Cor. 16:16)

For some people work is sheer drudgery. According to Evan Esar, 'All work and no play makes Jack a dull boy — and Jill a wealthy widow.' Another twist to the same story is seen in a statement by Aldous Huxley (1894-1963), the naughty novelist and critic. 'Like every man of sense and good feeling,' Huxley avowed, 'I abominate work.'

Many people are like Huxley, allergic to work and content to suffer the allergy. It is only in Jesus Christ that work takes on any fundamental meaning. Although Christians are accused of having a Puritan work ethic, the Christian view of work is much older than Puritanism. Martin Luther summarized it when he claimed that 'a dairymaid can milk cows to the glory of God'.

The word for 'work' in the Greek New Testament is *ergon*. It is seen in scientific English as a unit of energy, an 'erg'. In fact, it also surfaces in our word 'en*ergy*', meaning literally 'in work'.

Our Greek term *ergon* or its verb form *ergazomai* turn up numerous times in the Corinthian correspondence. The following are just a few examples.

Paul described Timothy as one who was 'carrying on the work of the Lord' (1 Cor. 16:10). Later on in his postscript Paul spoke of Stephanas, the first Greek Christian, as typical of a whole class of people who 'join in the work, and labour at it' (1 Cor. 16:16). These godly examples prove the axiom: 'When people are serving, life is no longer meaningless.' First, work is *spiritual*. We work for God's glory.

Second, work can be *wasted*. Paul spoke of some Christians whose life work will go up in smoke when Christ judges (1 Cor. 3:13-15). This is like building a sand-castle with elaborate detail, only to have it erased by the tide.

Third, work for the Lord is *costly*. Paul claimed with no sense of false humility: 'We work hard with our own hands' (1 Cor. 4:12). Christians find work satisfying when they are serving the Lord. Recently I chatted with a much respected pastor in America, Dr Howard Sugden. He confessed to being seventy-five years old, yet he thrives on the preaching of the Word. What's more, his church of more than 2500 members is also thriving. For Howard Sugden preaching is hard labour, but it is a labour of love.

Fourth, work is also *rewarded*. 'Are you not the result of my work in the Lord?' Paul asked rhetorically (1 Cor. 9:1). Great churches are often simply a prolonged shadow of their famous preachers. For instance, Westminster Chapel in its prime during the fifties and sixties bore the imprint of Dr Martyn Lloyd-Jones (1900-1981). Surely every pastor worthy of the call would see his only reward in the spiritual prosperity of the church which he serves.

Fifth, work is *meaningful*. After explaining the resurrection hope, Paul concluded, 'Always give yourselves fully to the work of the Lord, because you know that your labour in the Lord is not in vain' (1 Cor. 15:58). One of our church members undertook to sew cushions for each of the 800 seats at Kensington. He and a few friends stitched them up in record time, esteeming the comfort of Christians to be worth the work.

Sixth, work is *possible* because of God's enabling. In that great *magna carta* of Christian work Paul wrote, 'And God is able to make all grace abound to you, so that in all things at all times, having all that you need, you will abound in every good work' (2 Cor. 9:8). Two of my former students have recently reappeared. Both are gifted and much-used evangelists and Bible teachers, although neither showed promise during student days. Their present fruitfulness is a magnificent testimony to God's enabling grace.

Finally, our work is *consistent* with our words. 'What we are in our letters when we are absent, we will be in our actions [works] when we are present' (2 Cor. 10:11). Christians are consistent by definition. Nowhere is that seen more clearly than in their work for the Lord.

God's work-force

Work eats up about one-third of our waking hours, and some
spend even more time in toil. When we lived in Germany, we
often heard the generalization that 'Germans live to work'. In
other lands work is regarded as a necessary evil – people
'work to live'. Although she did not invent this idea, Dorothy
L. Sayers (1893-1957) did put it succinctly. 'Work is not
primarily a thing one does to live, but the thing one lives to
do,' the author assessed. It is, or should be, the full expression
of the worker's faculties, the thing in which he finds spiritual,
mental and bodily satisfaction, and the medium in which he
offers himself to God.

Work is seen as a *practice of God's presence*. To the Colossian Christians Paul wrote, 'Whatever you do, whether in
word or deed [work] do it all in the name of the Lord Jesus'
(Col. 3:17). In their relationships Christians are advised by
John: 'Let us not love with words or tongue but with actions
[works] and in truth' (1 John 3:18).

Whatever a Christian does, it is designed to display God's
glory. Recently we spent a relaxing day with friends, driving
out into the Cotswolds for a picnic. Before we could go, however, our hostess dashed off to leave a cake for the neighbours. She is a model wife, a model of work for God's glory
and the good of others.

A second aspect of work is *proof of God's priorities*. Paul
commended Thessalonian believers for their 'work produced
by faith, your labour prompted by love' (1 Thess. 1:3).
Pastors and teachers are sent by God to 'prepare God's people
for works of service' (Eph. 4:12).

The effectiveness of a pulpit ministry is not only a large
listenership. It is also the activity of the Christians. This is the
reason for a variety of ministries in many biblically taught
churches. There is a broad-based Sunday School. Ladies'
ministries are complemented by men's fellowships. Even
senior citizens are embraced by such churches. All of these

ministries flow from the serious study of the Word of God. Christians are equipped for 'works of service', which prove the dynamic of the divine Word.

Finally, work is seen as the *product of God's providence*. Paul assured his spiritual children at Philippi, 'He who began a good work in you will carry it on to completion until the day of Christ Jesus' (Phil. 1:6). Not only does our word refer to the work of God, but God also 'knows your deeds' and he will 'repay each of you according to your deeds' (Rev. 2:19, 23). Work, then, is the product of our efforts and God's.

In olden days people were more aware of God's interest. When an author finished a book, he scrawled on the last page, '*soli Deo gloria*' — 'for the glory of God alone'. Many contemporary problems of productivity and payment could be solved if both management and labour glimpsed God's glory as the purpose for work.

33.
Greeting cards

'Churches in the province of Asia send you **greetings**. *Aquila and Priscilla* **greet** *you warmly'* (1 Cor. 16:19)
'All the brothers send you **greetings'** (1 Cor. 16:20)
'This **greeting** *in my own hand'* (1 Cor. 16:21)

Greeting is great business. Recently we had a rush of Russian greeting cards into the West. The strange twist to this tale is this: they are Christmas cards from a Communist land. (Is money the mother of compromise?)

Such slick expressions of goodwill are almost infinitely adaptable. Pass your driving test, and suitable cards are sent. If you are unwell, friends find cards which are sometimes more humorous than you feel. Recently we celebrated our silver wedding anniversary, and our memories are piled up in a mound of cards on the window sill.

Since Victorian times cards have become synonymous with Christmas. Their use has grown from a trickle to a torrent. Now postmen do double rounds every December as they try to beat the deadline of Christmas Eve. At home we race to write cards to inadvertently forgotten friends.

Even the New Testament resembles a greeting card. The Greek word for 'greeting' is *aspazomai*. Although there are no easily identifiable reflections of this word in English, the idea of greeting is universal. In Greek it embraced a whole range of emotions, such as 'welcome, cherishing, remembrance, kissing, acclaim and homage'.

Paul's postscript to the Corinthian letter is a veritable greeting card. First, he sends greetings from the *churches in Asia* (1 Cor. 16:19). Most obviously he points to the Ephesian Christians, with whom he is enjoying a great time of growth (1 Cor. 16:8-9).

In German Baptist churches it is customary for Christians to give greetings from other fellowships. During the service visiting believers stand and give greetings from their home church. Then the local church commissions the visitors to return the greetings. It is a good custom which binds together the German Christians.

Second, Paul passes on greetings from *friends in Asia* (1 Cor. 16:19). Aquila and Priscilla had extended hospitality to Christian churches in Rome (Rom. 16:5). Later they also took the church at Ephesus into their home which probably was enlarged by the inclusion of a tentmaker's workshop (1 Cor. 16:19). During the first phase of gospel expansion there were no church buildings, and the Christians often congregated in homes (Col. 4:15; Philem. 2).

In our day this practice is emerging in the house-church movement, a development which presents problems to many biblically based believers. However, a more healthy renaissance is the emergence of Bible study and prayer groups in homes. These are a lively fact of life in many strong evangelical churches in Britain. The seed has grown into an enormous tree of blessing in such places as Korea, China and the United States. During the week Christians meet in homes under lay leadership, and on the Lord's Day they gather in a centrally located church for a great time of teaching, praise and worship.

The third expression of greetings is from *all the brothers* (1 Cor. 16:20). Christians are encouraged to give a 'holy kiss'. It seems significant that brothers greet brothers with a kiss. This was seen by Origen as a sign of mutual forgiveness, doing away with all grudges. It also combatted the cliques which plagued Corinthian Christians. It was carefully defined as a 'holy kiss' to avoid any sexual overtones. The New Testament advocated this holy kiss in several situations (for instance, Rom. 16:16; 2 Cor. 13:12).

In many countries this holy kiss is still seen. A friend returned from Russia some years ago. He recounted how gigantic Russian men had kissed him. When they pressed their bearded faces to his smooth one, my friend said it was like plunging your chin into a bird's nest. The experience was not completely pleasant, but the sentiment was heart-warming.

Finally Paul took the pen and appended *personal greetings* (1 Cor. 16:21). Paul's signature authenticated the epistle, which he had probably dictated to a companion. Paul may have used a secretary because of his failing eyesight or simply because of his work-load. Several letters indicate that Paul signed them personally (Gal. 6:11; Col. 4:18; 2 Thess. 3:17). A similar situation is seen in modern life. After dictating a letter to a typist, the writer signs the letter. A colleague of mine in America always adds a hand-written note, which I read first. Perhaps the Corinthians did the same.

God's welcome mat

Welcome is usually a glad greeting, but I recall one time when a welcoming party was decidedly unwelcome. After our wedding we finally fled into the hot July night. An hour later we drew up in front of a motel in suburban Detroit. Unfortunately, we mistook the manager's smile, thinking it was a knowing glance for newly-weds. When he ushered us into our room, a welcoming party of college friends was waiting. Their greeting was warm, but their welcome was not appreciated.

Greeting in the New Testament is always positive. Our Greek word is a *general term for friendship*. Most apostolic epistles end with this idea. In Romans Paul passes on greetings to seventeen families and friends (Rom. 16:2-16). To the Philippians Paul gives greetings from Caesar's bodyguard, or at least the Christians among them (Phil. 4:22). Even the little letter to Philemon is liberally laced with greetings (v.23-24). After the heady heights of Hebrews teaching there come greetings (Heb. 13:24). Peter, too, pens greetings in the Pauline mould (1 Peter 5:13-14), as does John in his epistles (2 John 13; 3 John 14).

Although I seldom preach away from my own church, whenever I do, people send greetings. Professional people who studied in Bristol pass on greetings to old friends. Retired folk ask to be remembered to Christian companions of earlier years. It all reminds me of the wide embrace of God's grace.

A second meaning of greeting is *to visit*. In the book of Acts Paul was always planning visits. When Paul touched the port of Caesarea, he first of all 'went up and greeted' the church (Acts 18:22). On his last journey he also stopped at Ptolemais (now known as Acre) where he 'greeted the brothers and stayed with them for a day' (Acts 21:7).

If a written greeting is welcome, a visit is even better. One of my dearest friends is pastor in a large town nearby. Nothing gives me greater joy than a visit from him and his family. It is as good as a day off. Our whole family looks forward to frequent feasts of friendship.

The third meaning of greeting is *a letter*. To the Colossians Paul wrote, 'I, Paul, write this greeting in my own hand' (Col. 4:18). The Thessalonians also had an autograph of the apostle. In fact, Paul wrote, 'I, Paul, write this greeting in my own hand, which is the distinguishing mark in all my letters' (2 Thess. 3:17). If first-edition books are cherished, think how those churches must have held on to letters signed by Paul himself.

Many members of our congregation are writers of encouraging letters. However, one couple stands out in my mind. She was terminally invalided, and he was nearly eighty, when I came to Bristol. Nevertheless, their letters of encouragement remain etched on my memory as a mark of Christian affection. Their lack of formal education was more than offset by the eloquence of love for the Lord and his servants.

Greetings are godly. They arise from Christian concern and express enduring attachments. It is therefore appropriate that this little book should end with the words of Paul:

'All the churches of Christ send greetings' (Rom. 16:16).